D0710994

THREE
BALL
DIGEST

"THREE BALL DIGEST

All you'll ever need to know about juggling three balls

By *DICK FRANCO*

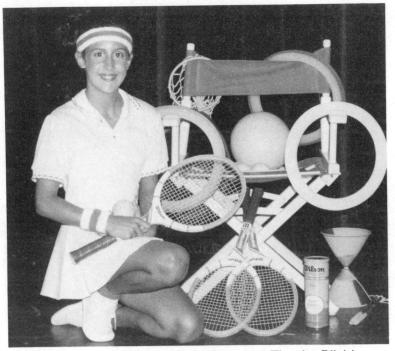

Photo Research by - Noel Francis   Thanks Blick!

Edited and Designed by -*Dick Franco*
Cover Photographs - Jay Freeman and Ivano Corazza
Proof Read by - Carlene Francis
Wiener dog Trainer - Sara Weaver
Macintosh Consultant - Jules Lauve
Diagrams by - Dick Franco
Paste ups & reductions by - Carlene Francis

brian dubé, inc.

Copyright 1989 by *Dick Franco*

All rights reserved.

No part of this book may be reproduced or utilized in any form or by any means, electronic or mechanical, including photocopying, recording, or by any information storage and retrieval system, without permission in writing from the publisher.

DESIGNED BY *DICK FRANCO*

Published in the United States by *brian dubé, inc.*
Manufactured in the United States of America.

Library of Congress Cataloging in Publication \ Data
Franco, Dick, 1952

"Three Ball Digest"
1. Juggling. I. Title.
GV1558.F73 1989   793.8'7   89-11769

ISBN 0-917643-05-4 Hardcover
ISBN 0-917643-04-6 Paperback

First printing September 1989

This book is dedicated to the memory of friend, fellow juggler, and all around nice guy Mr. Ludwig Mayer, better known as *Bobby May* - <u>The International Juggler.</u>

The Great
BOBBY MAY

<u>ACKNOWLEDGMENTS</u>

Joe Sullivan
Bobby May
Paul Bachman
Tom Cantone
Hans Kennon
The Trump Castle Crew
Ken Benge
Mr. Koma Zuru
Kris Kremo
Lloyd Timberlake
Gus Lauppe
Lindsay Leslie
El Gran Picaso
Sergei Ignatov
Johnny Aladdin
Alan Howard
Rudy Coby
The Raspyni Bros.
Bill Giduz and The IJA

CONTENTS

THREE: Routines

FOUR : Mastering the Head Roll

FIVE : Conclusion

You are about to be introduced to an ancient art form!

Ancient Terra Cotta Statue - Thebes 200 B.C.

The earliest documentation of juggling dates back to the time of Ptolomaer of ancient Thebes 200 B.C.

FOREWORD
By Alan Howard

Three ball juggling is the foundation for all other toss juggling. If you are going to be a juggler, this is the stuff you will need to know. Everything else you go on to learn will be derived from the basics with 3 balls. Used either as exercises leading up to other varieties of juggling, or as an end in themselves, the three ball lessons included in this book will provide you with an education as well as entertainment.

While many people continue on to explore the manipulation of other numbers or shapes, the simple juggling of three balls is a worthy goal in and of itself. A three ball routine is arguably the purest, most elemental form of juggling. As such, the performer using three balls is able to display his or her personality more effectively than while juggling larger items or a greater number of props. There is more room for individual expression. The audience can better relate to the performer as a person when there are fewer objects cluttering up the air between them. Three ball juggling allows you a freedom for motion, and emotion.

Dick Franco, a juggling historian as well as a top rated performer, has compiled the most comprehensive collection of three ball juggling variations to date. This book will be an invaluable guide to the possibilities of juggling, and should serve as an inspiration for the creation of your own moves and variations. Have fun!

Alan Howard   Cleveland, Ohio April 1989

Dick And Carlene Franco being presented with the "Silver Clown" Award by Princess Grace of Monaco at the 7th Monte Carlo International Circus Festival.

ABOUT THE AUTHOR

Dick Franco first learned to juggle in 1970 at Youngstown, Ohio. He was taught by his life long pal *Joey Sullivan*. A direct product of the I.J.A., Dick has just celebrated his fourteenth year as a show business professional and at this writing is one of the world's most talented and popular jugglers. His career was well established after he completed five consecutive world tours with the "Harlem Globetrotters" which took him to fifteen countries on four continents.

Dick got off the Globetrotter bus after their tour of France where he continued on with a story book style three and a half year tour of Europe. He worked Europe's most prestigious night spots and highlighted his tour by winning the Circus World Championships juggling competition not just once, but twice! Then, in 1980 Princess Grace of Monaco presented him with the prestigious "Silver Clown" award for his stunning performance at the 7th Monte Carlo Circus Festival of Monaco.

Dick is now a Las Vegas and Atlantic City regular where he has appeared at the Flamingo, Frontier, Bally's, Tropicana, Aladdin, Caesar's, Hilton, Playboy, Harrah's, Trump Plaza, and Trump Castle. He has enjoyed the distinction of being the only act ever nominated three times as Atlantic City "Entertainer of The Year", and is currently the longest running variety act in Atlantic City entertainment history. At this writing, Dick is starring with his hilarious comedy act in the Trump Castle award winning show "Glitter".

Dick has appeared on more than twenty major television shows all over the world and was a featured guest on ABC TV's "That's Incredible" where he juggled three, four, and then five ping pong balls using only his mouth. Dick is also becoming popular in films such as the recent one hour made for TV film "Juggling", and was also the narrator and major contributor to the film documentary about his friend and mentor, *Bobby May,* titled "Bobby May - A Great American Juggler". Dick has also helped design routines of a number of well known juggling artists such as *Carter Brown* and *Alan Howard*, and is the person credited with launching the career of juggling wiz kid *Anthony Gatto*. Dick is currently working on an act for his daughter Noel.

Dick's instructional qualifications are also very high. During his college years in Ohio, his "Juggling and Circus Techniques" classes were the most popular activity on campus! He has authored many articles on juggling and his current, first of a kind instructional book on juggling, "Three Club Juggling" is a very popular title. "Three Ball Digest" is the second book in a multivolume series of matched books which, when completed, will cover all popular forms of juggling in specialized detail, becoming the world's first comprehensive encyclopedia on the art of juggling. Each topic will be covered from the beginning stages all the way through to the most advanced variations. As an added extra, each book will contain a great many rare photographs from the *Dick Franco* archives and *Bobby May's* personal collection.

INTRODUCTION

The three ball cascade, although the simplest pattern of three object juggling, is quite difficult to learn without instruction. Most people who try to juggle three balls have no idea what the mechanics of a cascade consist of. Without instruction, most people make little progress and after a few disastrous tries, give up in frustration. I have run into the occasional person who picks up three balls for the very first time and just starts juggling, but I can tell you they are few and far between.

Jugglers, even novice jugglers, are a very select group of people. I believe that this is primarily true due to the difficulty in understanding the mechanics of the basic cascade pattern.

I have been an expert juggler for many years, but I remember it took three days of hard work before my teacher, *Joe Sullivan,* finally had me juggling three balls. I tried many different methods before I finally got it. The first time I got the cascade going, I could see it happening in front of me, but I had no idea why it was happening. Then it was many hours before I was able to do it again. Gradually though, I caught on, and after a few more days I had near perfect control. From then on I learned quickly, but before I tried something I would map out the mechanics of what I wanted to do on a piece of paper from my point of view, so I could visualize what I was about to do. This was a tremendous aid to me.

Everyone's ability to translate printed information into muscular coordination is different. Some people will read this instruction and be cascading in five minutes. Most will take longer and some will have great difficulty. One thing is for sure though, once you get the basic pattern, the rest will come easier.

Desire to learn is most important. **Dedication** is second. **Focus** is third. You need to focus your attention! You must focus on what you are ***doing right***, and also what you are ***doing wrong***, in order to make the proper corrections.

Once you have learned some basic tricks in juggling it becomes difficult to think of new things to do unless you happen to be able to practice with other jugglers. I have listed a great many three ball tricks in this book to give you an idea of the myriad of variations that can be done with just three balls.

You don't need to juggle nine balls to be considered a great juggler. Some of the most beautiful juggling routines I have ever seen are performed by three ball jugglers. Three current greats who come to mind are *Kris Kremo* , *Michael Moschen*, and *Peter Davison,* whose three ball routines are truly works of art. *Bobby May* and *Bela Kremo* were the masters of their day. *Paul Bachman's* comedy routine is classic! There is a great theatrical value to doing three balls in that the moving props provide an ever changing frame for facial expression and performance personality.

The beginning instruction of this book will be in great detail. Once you have reached a fair level of control over the basics, by all means skip around the intermediate and advanced chapters and try any of the easier tricks listed in each category.

Later in the book, as an added plus, I have included in depth instruction of one of my favorite tricks, the head roll. The head roll requires no toss juggling skill at all so get started on the basics exercises as soon as you can. It is quite difficult and will take time to learn.

Important Suggestions

For about the first two weeks, or at least until the basic cascade pattern with three is well under control, it is advisable to practice in short sessions, many times per day, such as 20 minutes, four to six times per day. As your endurance and concentration improve, increase the length of your sessions and decrease their number until you arrive at a schedule that is comfortable for you, yet still demonstrates that you are making definite progress from week to week.

Most sports are performed right or left handed. This is definitely not the case with juggling. The worst enemy of a juggler is his "bad side". Therefore, it is of great importance to over-practice one's "bad side" in order to make the most efficient progress. It is advisable to warm up the bad side first and spend as much time as is necessary per move to allow equal control to both sides. I have always had to work harder on my left side than my right, so as the old saying goes, I'd give my right arm to be ambidextrous!

Progress among jugglers varies greatly from person to person. A move that is mastered by one juggler in a few days may take weeks for another juggler to learn. Some professional jugglers have spent several years to getting a particular trick stage ready. For the beginner, visible progress should occur at least every third day.

Sometimes a particular move may show little progress even after many days of hard practice. Often, a trick like this may come easier if left alone for a few days. For me, progress has usually been obvious on the third day. Many times my first day on a new trick is fair, the second day a bit worse, and on the third day noticeable improvement.

It's a good idea to keep a wet towel handy to wipe hands, face, and props with occasionally. You will have a better grip with clean props. Practice in an area where you can pick up the balls easily, away from furniture that a ball could roll under.

Patience is also very important. You will not become a great juggler over night. Relax, concentrate, and let it happen. Juggling will become an enjoyable and challenging experience!

Note:
Terminology - Since there has never been a concise guide to naming tricks, I have taken it upon myself to name many of the moves contained in this book and have used as many commonly known terms as possible.

Another Note:
This book assumes the reader will have any of a variety of problems in learning the basic three ball cascade. Some common problems are addressed and solutions offered.

Yet Another Note:
Instruction in this book is intended for right handers. For left handers, reverse the procedures. Diagrams are from *your point of view.*

CHOOSING A GOOD PROP

The choice of the correct juggling prop is always an important decision. There are a number of excellent props that I can suggest for learning three balls which will also serve you well if you should later decide to work on four, five, or more objects.

I think that for the absolute beginner, bean bags are the best. They mold to the hand, don't bounce, and won't roll much so if you're juggling in the house, bean bags will cause a minimum amount of damage. There are many types of bean bags so I would suggest you find some that are as round as possible. These are usually made from at least six crescent shaped panels sewn together into a ball shape, and then stuffed. Many bean bag makers use beans or bird seed. I would suggest a filler of plastic pellets or some water-proof substance so that you can wash them without worry of them sprouting or getting soggy.

If you can't find or afford to buy bean bags, you can try making them yourself, or easier yet find some old, worn tennis balls to fill. Cut a one quarter inch slit somewhere on the ball and start pushing pellets in. Tennis balls are the right size for juggling, but really too light to be a good prop. You can make them heavier by filling them with a variety of things. Beans, BB's or bird shot are easy to find, but plastic pellets are certainly the best. Be sure to stuff them full so that the filling doesn't rattle around, then stitch or glue the slit so nothing falls out. Another good filler is heavy sheet plastic such is used for plastic table cloths. You can cut long, one inch wide strips of this and press it into the slit with a screw driver. Fill the ball completely then seal up the slit.

Another good "dead" ball is a street hockey ball which is available at most sporting goods stores. Although they do roll, they are just the right size for juggling, and also come in bright colors. They are a bit light though and need filling. Use the same procedure as the tennis balls.

If you want to start right out with a ball that bounces, the easiest to find is the solid rubber dog ball which can be found at any pet shop. A two and one quarter inch dog ball is just the right size and weight for learning to juggle, so start looking because later on you will need a ball of this type for the bounce tricks.

The best inexpensive ball is the white lacrosse ball which is also available in bright orange. Lacrosse balls are easy to find in Canada but quite hard to come by in the USA, however, you can get them from:

Brian Dube' Inc.
25 Park Place
New York, New York 10007
(212) 619-2182

The latest item of juggling technology and by far the absolute best of any ball to use for juggling is the molded silicone juggling ball. They come in various sizes and a good selection of neon, UV sensitive colors as well as bright white. They bounce like crazy and are the best for "English" and "effect" tricks. Silicone balls are quite expensive, but really the ideal prop for the serious juggler. They are also available from Brian Dube' Inc.

Whatever ball you choose, buy at least six or seven of them so you will have one or two to lose and five to work with when you decide to try larger numbers. Get at least one ball in a different color. It will come in handy as a marker ball when you are having trouble with a trick. Don't use the same three balls all the time. Rotate them so they break in evenly and feel the same.

LET'S GET STARTED !

ONE

LEARNING THE THREE BALL CASCADE

One Ball Exercises

It can't get any easier than this! Start with one ball in your right hand, with both forearms parallel to the ground and elbows at your sides. Plant your feet and don't move them! Throw the ball up and to your left hand in an arc that peaks about twelve inches above your eye level. The ball should land in your left palm without reaching the left hand forward or to your left. On the ideal throw, the catching hand should not move from this position. Don't reach up to catch the ball! Let it fall down to your hand and catch it at about waist level.

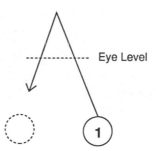

The One Ball Throw

Next, throw the ball back from left to right making sure you follow the same line of throw, up and over, twelve inches above eye level, to a catch in the right hand. Repeat this procedure back and forth many times until you have consistent throws from each hand

and consistent, comfortable catches made at waist level, without reaching up, forward, or to the side, and without stepping to make the catch. Keep your feet planted!

As soon as you have fair control over the one ball throw, start making higher and lower throws keeping your catches the same at waist level with elbows at the sides. This will help to improve your control, but keep in mind that the ideal throwing height is twelve inches above eye level. If you are not having any problems with this, go on to the next lesson.

Help:

If you are having problems, it is probably that you are throwing the ball either forward in front of you or back over your shoulder. If your hand is in the correct starting position, the ball must go exactly vertical on the plane in front of you in order to land correctly in the palm of the opposite, correctly positioned hand. Try facing close to a wall using the wall as a vertical reference point. If your hands in starting position are six inches from the wall, the ball at it's peak should also be six inches from the wall. If it's not, you're throwing too far forward or backward, so adjust your vertical throw angle accordingly.

Another thing you can do which is very effective, especially when teaching young children to juggle, is have a friend stand on a chair behind and directly above you. Get on your knees and put your legs between the chair legs. Have your friend bend forward so his or her hands are directly above yours when in the starting position. Throw the ball up from your right hand to your friend's left hand to be caught, and then dropped down to your left hand. Then, do the same starting with your left hand, throwing to your friend's right hand and dropping to your right hand. Your friend can tell you if you're throwing it straight up or not. This method will also help you later when you get to the two and three ball cascade. You should throw the ball a bit higher when using the friend method, but remember when practicing alone to throw from hand to hand through an equal, opposite arc that peaks about twelve inches above eye level.

Practice this until you can do ten perfect and consistent throws.

The Two Ball Cascade

Start with one ball in each hand, say with a white ball in the right hand and a color ball in the left. You will throw each ball to one of two points twelve inches above eye level.

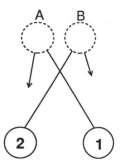

The Two Ball Cascade Pattern

Throw the white ball up to point A. Just as it peaks, throw the color ball up and *UNDER* the white ball to point B, catch the white ball in your left hand, then catch the color ball in your right, and STOP.

The exchange in the left hand takes place quite fast, so this is really the tricky part. It's very important that the color ball passes *UNDER* the white ball, so the throw with the left hand must be made just after the white ball peaks. If the white ball doesn't go high enough, or if your left throw is late, you will have a hard time making the left catch. Also each throw must reach the same height and fol-low an equal and opposite pattern. You should not be reaching for-ward or to the side to make the catches, and VERY IMPORTANT, don't reach up to catch the ball. All catches should be made at waist height. Try this a few times and if you are having trouble, take the trick apart and examine the mechanics of just what is happening.

Help:

Ask a friend to stand in front of you to lift the balls from your hands and pass them slowly through the pattern so you can see what should happen in slow motion, then get back to the starting position and try again. You can also have your friend stand on a chair behind and above you as explained before, then throw the balls up for your friend to catch, or you can use the wall technique.

Maintaining an EVEN TEMPO is very important in juggling. The tempo of this move is should be a very metronomish THROW-THROW-CATCH-CATCH. Again, if you are having trouble, take the trick apart mechanically and remember your priorities. Your first priority is the right throw, then the left, then the left catch, then the right catch. As you practice, isolate each move in your mind and focus on the important part of each move individually. At first you will find that you are thinking too slow, but don't worry, with practice, your brain will catch up.

Two Ball Exercises

At first keep these exercises to the throw-throw-catch-catch-STOP cycle and always start with the balls in the correct starting position, white right, and color left. Once you have a fair amount of confidence with one pass of the first cycle, try higher throws anywhere from a few inches to a few feet higher. Next try lower throws. The object is to decide how high you want the ball to go and throw it there as accurately as possible, with control. That goes for both throws. Each throw must be equal and opposite. You must control the props, not them control you. Again remember not to reach up for the catches. Catch at waist level. Adjust your throws so you are not reaching forward, side, or back, and don't start stepping or walking to make a catch. Walking is a hard habit to break. If the ball comes down out of reach, keep your feet planted and let it go.

When you have fair control of the two ball cascade starting with the right hand, practice for a while starting with the left hand. You will throw left-right-catch-catch-STOP. Practice this just as much as you practice your right starts in order to develop a symmetrical pattern. Remember to keep an even tempo and try the higher and lower throws. If your left starts are worse than your right starts, practice them until you are equally confident starting on both sides.

Continuous Throws with Two Balls

Next, try continuous throws. Start as usual throwing right-left-catch-catch, but continue with a second pass, left-right-catch-catch, then again, right-left-catch-catch, left-right-catch-catch, and so on. Try to develop a nice even tempo, then "exercise" the pattern by doing it with high, and then low throws. As soon as you get good control of continuous throws, move on to three balls.

The Three Ball Cascade

If you have practiced the previous exercises well, you should have little trouble getting the three ball cascade going. There are a number of approaches toward learning this, but I think any approach used is easier if you have a clear picture of what is going to happen. Probably one of the best ways to visualize the mechanics of a three ball cascade is on a pool table. Get the one, two, and three ball, then mark two points about ten inches apart on the far side rail. Start with your hands about two feet apart with the one and three ball in your right hand and the two ball in your left. Roll the one ball first to the left mark with enough force that it rebounds slowly to the left hand. As the one ball bounces off the rail, roll the two ball from the left hand to the right mark on the rail with the same force. As the two ball hits the rail, you should be catching the one ball in your left hand. As the two ball rebounds, roll the three ball to the left mark. As it rebounds toward the left hand, roll the one ball again, then the two, then the three, and so on.

Let's start again with two white balls and one color. Put the color ball in the palm of the right hand, a white ball in the fingers of the right hand, and a white ball in the left hand. First, do a right hand start two ball cascade with the two white balls throwing right-left-catch-catch-STOP. Repeat this many times letting the color ball sit in your palm for a few passes. Catch on the right using only the fingers of the right hand.

Now try the third throw. Starting with two balls in the right hand, throw the right, white ball first, then the left. As the left, white ball peaks, throw the color ball under the descending white ball and over to a catch in the left fingers, and STOP. You should now have a white ball in your right hand, a white ball in your left palm, and a color ball in your left fingers. Rearrange the balls back to the right starting position and repeat.

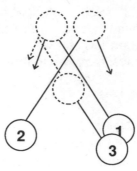

The Three Ball Cascade

Repeat this procedure until all three of your throws are reaching the same height and you are catching comfortably without excessive reaching.

Help:

If you are having trouble seeing the cascade pattern try the technique explained earlier. Ask a friend to stand in front of you to lift the balls from your hands and pass them slowly through the pattern so you can see what should happen in slow motion, then get back to the starting position and try again. You can also have your friend stand on a chair behind and above you as explained before, then throw the balls up for your friend to catch, hold briefly, and then drop back down to you. Be sure to throw your right hand throws to your friend's left hand and your left hand throws to his right.

If you are lucky enough to know someone who can already juggle, here's a great helper. Stand with your left side snug against your friend's right side. Tuck your touching arms behind your backs. Your right hand will start with the two balls, your friends already trained left hand will have one ball. You start the cascade from the right. Since your friend can already juggle, he or she will know what to do with that first ball when it comes and be able to correct any mistakes you are making with your first throw. Your friend will make all of the left throws and you will make the rights. When your right arm finally kicks in, switch sides and do the same exercises for your left arm. This only works if your friend can already cascade three balls!

If you are really having trouble getting the cascade going and none of the above suggestions have worked for you, try following the same instruction using three light scarves. They will travel slower through the air and allow you more time to react.

BASIC EXERCISES

The act of just trying the various tricks in the following lessons will in itself greatly improve your basic cascade, so don't worry if you don't have total control of the pattern. After you have worked on these basic cascade exercises for a while, by all means continue on and try some of the easier tricks at the beginning of each of the following chapters.

1. Start the cascade. Push each throw gradually higher and higher up to about three feet above your head, then gradually lower and lower until the pattern is as low as possible, then back up to normal height.

2. Start the cascade. Pick one right hand throw and toss it to peak about three feet above your head. Let it bounce once. As it peaks after the bounce and begins downward, recover the cascade by starting with your left hand. Repeat this exercise throwing the high throw from the left hand and recovering with the right.

3. Start the Cascade. Pick one right hand throw and toss it to peak about three feet above your head. As It starts downward, before it bounces, recover the cascade by starting with your left. Repeat with the high throw coming from the left.

4. Combine all of these. For example, start the cascade, spread it out to higher throws, then compress gradually to a short low cascade, then toss one high let it bounce and continue, then toss one high, no bounce, and continue.

Once you can get through this series of exercises a few times without missing, move on to the next section.

YOUR FIRST BASIC TRICKS

One-up, Two-up

This is an easy, great looking trick. Start with two balls in the right hand and one in the left. Throw the first right ball straight up on the center line of your body. As it peaks, throw the outer two balls in unison straight up on the outsides of the center ball. Catch the center ball with the right hand and throw it straight back up again between the two descending balls. Spread your hands to catch in unison the two descending balls, throw them straight back up, and so on.

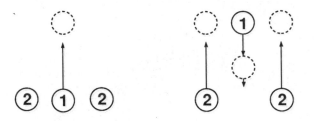

One-up, Two-up

Start with just two throws and stop, then go for more throws until you can reach ten throws. You will notice that your left hand is just throwing the same ball up and catching it while the right hand is juggling two balls in separate columns. When you get good control starting with the right, switch and start with the left. You will then be juggling two in columns with the left hand, and the same ball up and down with the right.

Once you have fair control of this move, try starting with a cascade, then throw one ball up the middle and go into the one-up, two-up trick. After a few passes, go back into the cascade by starting with either hand when the single ball is peaking.

One-up, Two-up - Cross

Start out the same as the regular one-up, two-up. Make a few passes of it then try to make the two balls which are thrown in unison cross in mid-air. To do this, hook your hands outward somewhat throwing the right ball slightly higher than the left ball, then reach inward to catch the single ball. Throw both balls at the same time, but push the right ball just slightly higher so as to avoid collision of the two and still result in a unison catch.

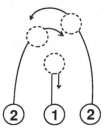

One-up, Two-up, Cross

Throw the cross in every so often when you are working on the regular one-up two-up, then try to recover your normal cascade by starting with either hand while the single ball is in the air.

Half Shower Right & Left

The half shower is an easy trick. Start your regular cascade. Notice that each newly thrown ball goes *UNDER* the descending ball. Pick any right hand throw, hook your arm outward slightly and throw one ball *UP* and *OVER* the descending ball.

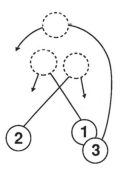

The Half Shower

Try random over the top throws with your right hand, recovering the cascade each time, then try some from the left. Work on each side until they are equal on random throws, then try alternating by throwing the color ball over the top each time it comes to either hand.

Next, go for every throw from the right hand, or "solids". Start the cascade for a few throws, then throw every right hand throw over the top, then switch and throw "solids" from the left.

Try to maintain as even a tempo as possible, then go for a broken tempo by throwing the over the top throws higher than the other throws. The tempo will break because you have to wait for the higher throw to come down.

Double Shower or Reverse Cascade

This is a great looking trick! It's easy because its just "solid" right and left throws, all over the top. Start the cascade then starting with the right, throw two consecutive throws, right, left, then recover the cascade. Try this a few times, then go for three consecutive throws, right, left, right, then four consecutive, right, left, right, left, and so on. Practice this until you can do twenty-five consecutive over the top throws.

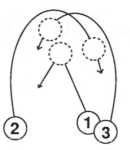

The Double Shower or Reverse Cascade

Under the Wrists

Start with one ball in the right hand. Bring your left arm part way across your chest so that your left hand is in the middle of your body and roughly twelve inches from your chest. Take your right hand *UNDER* the left wrist and throw straight up just in front of your left elbow. Uncross your arms and catch the ball in the left hand.

Next, repeat the move with your left hand, bringing your right arm across your chest and throwing under the right wrist, straight up, uncross your arms and catch. Work the ball back and forth with under the wrist throws building a smooth pattern with a quick, even tempo.

Now get two balls, one in each hand. Bring the right ball under the left wrist for the straight up throw. Toss the left ball straight up the middle column, uncross your arms and catch. Bring the left ball under the right wrist for the straight up throw. Toss the right ball straight up the middle column, uncross your arms and catch. Practice this cycle of under the wrist throws until the pattern becomes fluid, then continue.

Start a regular cascade using the color ball. After a few cycles of the pattern, go for one under the wrist throw when the color ball comes to the right hand. You will notice that when making the under the wrist throw from right to left that your left hand tends to get in the way. It will help if you make that left catch a little higher than usual to allow the right hand easier passage underneath. Likewise with the right. Just after you commit to making a right throw under the wrist, raise your left hand and make the next left catch more of a snatch up of the ball. Bring it up a few inches, bending your elbow so your hand moves in toward your chest. This will leave you plenty of room to get the right throw past. Practice this technique on random under the wrist throws from both sides, then go for two and more consecutive from each side. When you think you are ready, start to build consecutive throws from both right and left beginning with just two, right, left, and working up to more.

One Between Two or Back and Forth

This trick can be a bit confusing to learn. Start with two balls in the right hand and one in the left. Throw the first right ball in a low arc to the left hand, before you catch left, throw the left ball straight up to a height of about two feet, catch the incoming ball and quickly toss it back in a low arc to the right and catch the ball now descending left. Before you catch right, throw the right ball straight up about two feet, catch the incoming ball, again quickly tossing it in a low arc back to the left and so on.

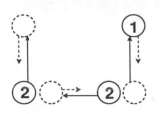

<u>One Between Two or Back and Forth</u>

What is actually happening is the right ball and left ball are just going straight up and down in columns while the center ball is being tossed back and forth in a low arc. If you find this confusing, make the center ball the color ball. It will be your first throw and be the only ball traveling back and forth from hand to hand.

Under the Leg

At first this will seem difficult, but as you learn to get your balance and anticipate the under the leg throw, it will get easier.

Start the regular cascade. Your first under the leg throw will be from your right hand. As you cascade, shift your weight over to your left foot and lift your right heel so that just your right toe is touching the ground. Spread your cascade pattern out by throwing higher. This will give you a little more time to make the under the leg throw. Pick a right hand throw, lifting your right leg, bending at the knee, try to make the throw and recover the cascade. The timing should be just about right if you start to lift your leg just as you catch the ball that will go under it.

Work on this with random throws, recovering the cascade each time, then switch sides and develop your left under the leg throws.

Next try alternating right and left by throwing the color ball under the leg each time it comes to either hand. Then, try "solids" under the right leg, and then "solids" under the left leg. On "solids" your toe will just touch the ground lightly between throws to aid in keeping your balance, or maybe not at all if you can stand on one foot.

The Three Ball Shower

The three ball shower, or three in a circle, is a fairly difficult basic trick because it is not at all similar to a cascade. All of the throws are made from the right, all of the catches are made with the left, and each caught ball is handed from the left to the right hand.

Start with just two balls, one in each hand. Throw the right ball to the left hand so it peaks slightly above eye level. Just after you throw, hand the ball in your left hand over to your right. This is not a throw or a toss. It's a hand off! When you get the ball in your right hand, catch left. At the same time throw right again, and hand off again. The balls will travel round and round in a counter-clockwise direction.

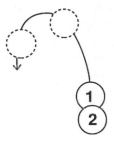

The Two Ball Shower

The three ball shower is a bit more difficult and will probably take some work to perfect. Start with two balls in the right and one in the left. The first two throws will be from the right. Both balls will have to leave your right hand before you can hand off the left ball. You have to throw quickly and pass quickly, very quickly! Start out trying one revolution. Throw right, right, hand off, right, catch, catch, catch, STOP. If the balls are coming down too fast, make your right hand throws higher. It is very important that all the right hand throws reach the same height, otherwise you will have trouble catching them individually, and still have enough time to hand them off.

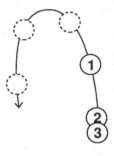

The Three Ball Shower

Work on one revolution until it feels comfortable, then go for four throws, five, and so on. Most people reach an impasse at about ten throws. Keep practicing. It takes time to develop the speed necessary to do a good three ball shower. Once you can get to ten throws every time, practice spreading the pattern out higher, and then wider. Next, start with a cascade, blend into a shower, spread it out higher, then wider, then get back into the cascade by throwing a left under any descending ball.

One Up - Two Up Spread

This is the same trick as the one up-two up you learned earlier except that the single ball goes in a column to the right or left of the two columns the unison balls are traveling in.

Get into your regular one up-two up pattern. Take the single ball, carry it under and out of the middle column and throw it up on the outside, right column. You now have two balls going up and down in unison in the left two columns and one ball going up and down by itself in the right column. You are still juggling two balls in your right hand and two in your left. It's just the order of the columns that you've rearranged. As you get better control of the spread pattern, start to widen it out as far as you can. Make as much space as you can between the two left columns and the right column.

One Up - Two Up Spread Changing Places

Start your one up-two up spread so that the single ball is in the outside, right column. Make a few cycles of the pattern, then toss the single ball up and over the right unison ball and into the middle column. Repeat a few cycles there, then toss the single ball up and over the left unison ball and into the left column. Reverse the procedure to get the single ball back to the middle again, then over to the right end again. Work towards a goal of moving the single ball constantly in and out of the three columns, right, middle, left, middle, right, middle, left, middle, and so on.

One Up - Two Up Spread - Changing Ends

Start your one up-two up spread so that the single ball is in the outside, right column. Make a few cycles of the pattern, then throw the single ball high up over the two unison balls so that it comes down in the left column to continue the pattern. You are now juggling two balls in your left and one in your right. Recover, then throw the single ball again up, over the pattern and back to the right column. Work on this until you can throw the single ball continuously over the top back and forth on every throw.

Next, try the same trick but instead of throwing the single ball over the top of the two unison balls, cross your arm with the single ball *UNDER* the pattern to make a straight up throw in the opposite end column.

A great effect with this trick is to purposely look in the opposite direction of the single ball throw. Watch the ball peripherally and turn your head in the direction opposite the travel of the ball.

Later when you've learned some of the more advanced variations in the following chapter, come back to this trick! Try it making the single ball change sides by throwing right and left back crosses or shoulder throws, behind the back passes, or under the leg passes. Don't forget to come back to this later!

Here's another exercise that you can use to help improve your dexterity!

Two Balls Rotating in the Palm

Take two balls and hold them loosely in the palm of your right hand. Manipulate the balls with your fingers so that they rotate smoothly and continuously in either a clockwise or counter-clockwise direction. Learn to do this with both hands simultaneously, then try rotating three in one hand.

Work on these basic tricks a great deal before going onto more difficult moves. They will establish a foundation for what is to come. The better you know the basics, the easier it will be to learn the more advanced variations. It's always a good idea to go through the full list of basic tricks at the beginning of your practice session. It will gently warm up your body and tune your reflexes so that you can get the most out of the rest of your rehearsal. Once your joints have loosened up, move on to the advanced tricks.

Dick Franco - Café Versailles New York 1982
(Photo H. V. Francis)

TWO

INTERMEDIATE

and

ADVANCED

Congratulations! You've reached the advanced section. The instruction from here on in will be minimal. Since you already know the basics, here are some tricks you can do using those basic skills!

CASCADE TRICKS

Clawing

Start a cascade. Pick any right hand catch. Instead of catching by having the ball land in the hand palm up, just as you release a right hand throw, turn the right hand over and SLAP down hard at the ball to be caught. Turn the hand over and continuo the cascade. Work on random right hand claws, then try the left hand. Next work on clawing the color ball each time it arrives left and right, then go for "solids" (every ball). The slap can be anything from soft and mild to fast furious, or a gradual transition from one to the other.

Here's a good exercise that will help you learn the clawing technique and also speed up your reflexes.

The Two Ball Claw Catch

Get two balls, one of them the color ball. Make a "V" with the index and second fingers of the right hand, holding the right hand out, palm down. First try a short toss from the right hand to a catch on the back of the fingers, palm down. Get comfortable with this finger catch, then put the white ball in the palm of your hand and the color ball on the fingers. Lift the right hand releasing both the white ball from the palm and the color ball from the fingers into the air at the same time. Quickly claw the upper, color ball into the palm of your hand, then move under to catch the white ball on the back of the fingers. You have to be very quick to make the change! Work on this with both hands. You can also use the two finger catch after throwing a single ball out of a cascade.

Rolls Off the Head or Place Rolls

Since you have already learned the downward slap in "clawing", let's try the upward slap. The upward slap will come in handy for a great many tricks.

Start the cascade. Pick any right catch. You will catch it palm up, normally, except that you will quickly snatch the ball upward and out of the pattern and place it on the crown of your head, slightly forward and slightly left of center. Quickly release it there and slap down to catch the ball that is already coming from the left. The ball on your head, if properly placed, will roll slowly off the left side of your head and down to your left hand. Just as the ball rolls off your head, throw from the left to continue the cascade. Be careful on the upward snatch! If you don't have a good grip on it, the ball will really go flying!

Work on the right random throws, then the left, then snatch the color ball every time it arrives right and left. Next, go for "solids" right, and "solids" left. Proper placement of the ball on the head can really make this trick easy. If you put it on just the right spot, it will balance momentarily and then roll slowly off to your catching hand. This will give you plenty of time to make the catches that follow.

Eating the Apple

Here's a great trick that works just the same as the place rolls on the head. Start with two balls and an apple. Each time the apple comes to the right hand, snatch it up, but instead of putting it on your head, put it up to your mouth, take a bite, then throw it back in the pattern without breaking tempo. You can bite every time it comes to the right hand or with both hands by snatching it up every time it comes to your right and left.

The Armpit Cascade

This is an easy, comical trick and nobody does it with more flair and style than *Paul Bachman.*

Start your cascade. Quickly place one right hand throw under your left arm pit and STOP. Next place the ball in your left hand under your right armpit. Reach your left hand across and take the ball out from your left armpit, then put the ball in your right hand under your left armpit, reach your right hand across and take the ball out from your right armpit, then put the ball in your left hand under your right armpit, then reach your left hand across and take the ball out from your left armpit, then place the ball in your right hand under your left armpit, and so on.

Do this as slow as you want at first. It's one of the few tricks in juggling that you can really take your time on. Then, speed it up for a really strange looking trick!

The Crossed Arms Reverse Cascade

The crossed arms cascade may seem difficult when you first try it. but once you understand what is supposed to happen you will find it almost as easy as a normal cascade.

Start with two balls in the right hand and one in the left. Cross your right arm under your left with the crossing point at about mid-forearm. The pattern will be a double shower or reverse cascade. The arms remain crossed at all times for both the throws and the catches. Throw the first ball from the right. The second ball from the left goes over the first ball, and the third ball over the second.

If this looks confusing, try just two throws with two balls. Cross your arms then throw right, left, catch, catch, and STOP. Make sure the second ball goes over the first. Then try left, right, catch, catch, and STOP. Go over this a couple of times and then try it with three balls again.

Next, try to get into the crossed arms, from a regular reverse cascade. Start the normal cascade, then go into the normal reverse cascade. Throw one right hand high over the top to the left hand. Quickly and completely cross your hands over and throw another right hand throw over to your left hand, and recover the reverse cascade with the arms crossed.

Chops

Chops is one of the best looking three ball tricks there is! To learn it, go back to "Your First Basic Tricks" and clean up the "under the wrists" trick. Work on it until you have a smooth, neat pattern of even tempo and can sustain at least ten consecutive right and left throws. That's every throw from both hands going under the wrist. Note while you practice that on each catch before the under the wrist throw, your catching hand moves up toward your chest, then back down through the pattern to make the throw under the wrist of the opposite hand. If you accentuate this same up and down motion just a bit more, you will be doing chops!

Start "solid" under the wrist throws. Watch your catches You should be reaching up slightly to snatch up the catch, bringing it toward your chest, then down and under your opposite wrist for the next throw. Gradually accentuate the upward snatch so that your hand comes up to forehead height, then chop down through the pattern and change direction to make the under the wrist throw. Try the chop motion on random catches, then go for alternating lefts and rights, then finally "solids".   If you push the under the wrist throws higher and gradually increase the distance of travel of the chopping motion, the pattern will slow down to the point that it will be quite easy to sustain. Widen the pattern, then chop down hard and fast to make a really dynamic trick.

One High - Switch Two

This is an easy trick. First learn the switch. Put one ball in each hand. Throw the right ball horizontally to the left hand at the same time you throw the left ball horizontally to the right hand. The right throw goes on top and the left throw goes on the bottom.

The throw is a quick, snappy action and immediately after the balls leave your hands, your right hand moves down and your left hand moves up to make the catch. Practice this switch until you can do it without looking.

Now start your cascade. Pick any right hand throw and toss it high. Make the switch once, then recover the cascade by starting with either hand. If you throw the ball higher and have a quick enough switch, you can switch two or three times before it comes down.

One High - Shower Two

This trick is similar to one high-switch two except that you will shower the two balls instead of switch them. You have already learned the two ball shower when you were practicing the basic tricks getting ready to do the three ball shower, so this should come easy.

Practice your two ball shower a bit. Get it as fast and tight as possible. Start a three ball cascade. Throw one ball high, then while it is in the air, shower the two balls once or twice around. You may have to look at the two ball shower to get it right. This is fine, In fact it makes the trick look better if you throw the single ball very high, look down to do the two ball shower, then look back up at the last second to recover the cascade!

The Snatch Up - Over and Drop

This trick is fairly complicated. Think of it as a half shower with over the top throws coming from the right hand, except that the ball that travels over the top will be snatched up, carried over, and dropped by you, instead of just being thrown over in an arc.

Start the cascade. Pick any right hand catch. Snatch up at the ball and carry it directly up, over, and across the pattern, then quickly drop the ball straight down to your left hand. You then have to get your right hand quickly back to slap down on the next right hand catch. This trick looks great when you snatch up every other ball that comes to the right hand.

Next, work on the left hand, then try the best looking way to do this trick, alternating left and right with the same ball. To do this, start by snatching up the color ball, drop it down to the left, snatch it back up with the left, over and drop it down to the right, then snatch it back up again with the right, and so on. The farther over you carry each ball, the better this trick will look.

Reverse Catches

The reverse catches are used by a great many professional jugglers. *Kris Kremo, Grigori Popovich,* and *Alan Howard* do it especially well.

First you have to understand the catching position of the hand. Hold your left hand out, palm down. Turn your hand over, palm up, in a *clockwise* direction. Believe it or not, this is the catching position. To throw you will turn your hand back to the normal throwing position. At first it may seem awkward, but in time you will find it easy to catch like this. Next do the same with your right hand. Your right hand will turn *counter clockwise.*

Now take one ball in your right hand. Toss it straight up about twelve inches, turn your hand completely around *counter clockwise* to catch the right ball. Turn your hand all the way back around so that you can make a normal throw and try again.   It may take you a few days to feel comfortable with this, but keep working on the one ball toss and catch on both left and right sides. Next toss the ball in a low arc from the right hand to a reverse catch in the left hand, turn your left hand over, then toss it normally back to a reverse catch in the right. Practice this with high throws, and also with low arcing, wide throws.

When you're comfortable with these throws and catches, start the three ball cascade. Pick any right or left hand catch and start making random reverse catches, recovering the cascade after each try. Next try alternating sides by reverse catching the color ball every time it arrives, then go for three or four consecutive catches on either side. "Solids" right or left are next, then solids with both hands so every catch is a reverse catch. It will take a lot of practice to get long runs with "solids" both hands. Set a goal of twenty-five and work towards it.

The Cascade on the Side - One Arm Behind the Back

If you are tall and thin with long arms, this trick should be a cinch for you. If your arms are short, or you're thick around the middle, you will have to work much harder to perfect this trick.

Start with two balls in your right and one in your left. Take your right arm and stretch it as far around behind your back as you can get it. Your right hand has to get all the way around so that it is next to your left hand. The cascade will happen on your left side, under your left arm pit. Get your right hand in place, then look down at your left side. If you can easily see your right hand from the wrist down, you're in good shape. If you can't, you're going to have some hard work ahead of you. Because of the confined space and limited movement, you have to keep the cascade pretty tight. Usually the hardest part is catching. If you are having trouble, try just two throws with two balls, starting first with the right and then with the left.

Once you get control of three balls in this manner, try getting into it from a regular cascade. Start the normal cascade. Throw one right hand throw high and quickly reach your right hand all the way behind your back. Your next throw will be from your left, but it will be a short throw to your right hand which is now stretched around behind your back to your left side. Make the catch left, throw a short right, and catch right. Continue the cascade in this position.

To get back to the normal cascade, throw one left hand throw high, up and over toward the right side of your body. Quickly, bring your right arm from behind your back to catch and recover the normal cascade in front of you.

Cascade on the Side - Alternating left and right.

This trick is one of the best looking three ball tricks ever invented. It is also very difficult! I've seen it used by *Kris Kremo* and *Alan Howard* in their stage acts and can tell you it always gets a great audience response!

You must have a good, strong side cascade on both the left and right sides, so work well on both before continuing.

Stretch your right arm behind your back and start the side cascade on your left side. Pick any left throw. Throw it high, up and over to the right side of your body. As it travels, uncross your right arm and quickly cross your left arm behind your back and over to the right side. Your right hand will throw a short throw to your left hand, then catch the descending ball. Continue the cascade in this posi-

tion. Next throw a high right throw back up and over to your left side.
Uncross your left arm, and quickly re-cross your right arm behind
your back to your left side, and again recover the cascade.

Practice towards being able to throw the color ball to the opposite side each time it comes to either your right or left hand. That
means you will throw two short throws, then a high throw on each
side.

Four Ball Like Three - Multiplex Cascade

This is a great looking trick that will have you juggling four balls
even if you don't know how! You already know the cascade, now go
to page 37 paragraph 4 and learn the multiplex throw. Put them
together like this. Put two balls in the left hand and two in the right.
Starting with the right, throw a single ball to the left hand, then throw
multiplex, both balls from the left hand, and then the last and single
ball from the right. The pattern is exactly the same as the regular
three ball cascade except that the two balls in the multiplex throw
travel together. In the beginning it will help to spread the pattern out
a little higher than normal to give you more time to make the multiplex catch.

UNDER THE LEG TRICKS

You've already learned the basic under the leg moves back in
the basics section. Here are some ideas for different variations using
the same skills.

1. Throw right throws under the left leg, and left throws under the
right leg. You have to reach a bit farther to get the ball under the
opposite leg.

2. Throw every other right throw under first the right leg, and then
the left leg. Also, throw every other left throw under first the left leg
and then the right leg.

3. Throw "solids" from the right hand alternating back and forth
under first the right and then the left. Work on the same from the left.
If you're trying to lose weight, this trick will help.

4. One of the most difficult under the leg tricks is "solids with both hands. For this trick you will be running in place lifting the knees as high as you can and throwing every ball under the leg. At the point of each throw, you will be completely off the ground for a split second. All right throws go under the right leg, and all left throws go under the left leg.

This is a killer trick to learn so start out with just two throws and work up adding one throw at a time. You can slow down the jumping somewhat by throwing the balls up to about eye level, but eventually you will find the easiest way to do this trick is with a short, low arcing toss. It will take a week or two to build up your jumping stamina, but once you get a ten throw run of this trick, I'm sure you will agree it is the ideal finish trick for any three ball routine.

SHOWER TRICKS

If your three ball shower isn't perfect by now, go back and work on it! Practice it going from normal height, to high, to wide, and then to as low and as fast as you can do it. Get it as near perfect as possible!

Three Ball Shower - Throwing Two Multiplex

This is an easy one. Let's start by learning the multiplex throw and catch. Take two balls in the right hand. Adjust them in your hand so they sit almost vertically one atop the other. Bend your wrist back slightly to get them vertical. Now, with as little wrist motion as possible, push the two balls up from the palm of your hand and over for a left hand catch, releasing them by opening the fingers. The two balls are thrown at the same time, but the main idea is to have them stay one over the other, but separate vertically by a few inches in the air, then fall down in the same order to be caught almost two at a time in the left hand.

Start with two balls in the right and one in the left. Make the first throw a multiplex throw to the left hand. Hand off the left single ball to the right, make a multiplex catch left, throw right, hand off multiplex to the right, catch left, throw multiplex from the right, and so on. This is just like the two ball shower, except for the second ball of the multiplex. You can go as slow as you want with this so it will be good practice for the next variation. As you practice, try to get the two balls of the multiplex throw to separate vertically as much as possible.

Next, start with two balls right, throw a multiplex throw to the left, pass the single ball off to the right. The two balls of the multiplex throw should be separated now and descending to your left hand. Reach your left hand up quickly, grab the bottom ball and continue with a regular shower pattern of normal shower throws. You will have a slight break in tempo on the grab. The farther apart the multiplex balls spread, the less of a break this will be.

Now start a regular three ball shower. Stop throwing from the right hand for one throw. Hand off one more ball from the left so that you collect a second ball in the right. Make one multiplex throw. When the multiplex throw comes down, get back into the regular shower pattern. Practice random multiplex throws, then every third, then every other.

Three Ball Shower - Over the Shoulder

The shower over the shoulder is a valuable trick because it's easy to sustain for many throws, and looks great if you do it while turning in a circle.

If you haven't learned the shoulder throw yet, you will find a description of it in the "Behind the Back" section.

First warm up with a few shoulder throws with one ball, throwing with the right hand, over the right shoulder so that the ball comes down to the left hand. Start a three ball shower. Pick any throw and make it a shoulder throw, then recover the shower. Work on random throws, then try every third, then go for "solids".

When you have good control of "solids", try turning one full revolution to your left. To do this, lead your left hand by throwing each ball slightly behind the normal catching point so that you have to turn slightly to your left to comfortably catch it. Make one revolution, then go directly back into the front cascade.

Three Ball Shower - Pass Behind the Back

Start the normal shower. Spread it out a bit higher than normal. Lean back slightly so you can bring the pattern closer to your chest. Throw two consecutive right throws high, then quickly hand off the left ball by passing it behind your back to your right hand, then recover the normal shower. As your hand off behind the back gets quicker, you will be able to lower your cascade pattern. Work on random throws, then every other, then go for the very difficult "solids". This same technique will work with a hand off under either leg.

Three Ball Shower - Reverse Direction

You already know the basic shower pattern throwing from the right and catching left. Reverse that method and learn to shower the other way, throwing from the left. Start with two balls in the left hand. This will probably feel quite awkward for a while. Work on the reverse direction shower until it's almost as good as your regular shower, then try going back and forth from one direction to the other without stopping.

Three Ball Shower - Back and Forth

If you have learned the reverse direction shower and can change directions back and forth, notice what happens at the moment when the pattern changes direction. There is one ball in each hand and one ball in the air above the right hand. When you change direction, the ball above the right hand, falls back down to the right hand, the ball that's in the right hand is passed back to the left hand, and the ball that was in the left hand gets thrown up and over to the right hand to start the shower in the other direction.

Do this! Get the color ball, make it the bottom ball on the right so that it's the second ball thrown from the right hand. Watch it go up and over, and to the left hand. Right after you pass it off to the right, change direction. As soon as the color ball is handed back to the left, change direction again. The idea is to keep the color ball handing back and forth between the hands, while the two outside white balls alternate going straight up and down in columns. This trick forms a "U" shaped pattern with the color ball going back and forth on a line along the bottom of the "U". Start out going back and forth only once, then go for more. If you widen the pattern out, the pass back and forth will turn into more of a direct toss than a hand off. The wider you make your pattern, the better this trick looks.

This is a great transition trick to put in a shower routine. Start out with a normal cascade, then go into a shower. Do three random behind the back passes, then go back into a shower in one direction for six throws, then reverse the direction for six throws, then back and forth for eight throws, then straight into "solids" over the shoulder, turning a full circle.

Three Ball Square Shower (pass over the top)

The square shower is an excellent audience trick, just because there is so much action taking place. Actually it is the same move as you learned back in the cascade section called "Snatch Up, Over and Drop", except that you do "solids" on one side only, so that all the snatches are done with the right hand and all the drops go to the left hand. Instead of handing off from the left to the right, you will have to toss up to your right hand. Go back to the cascade section for a description of "Snatch Up, Over and Drop".

The Statue of Liberty

If you can do the square shower well, you are very close to doing the Statue of Liberty trick. Start the square shower, then gradually raise your right hand a little on each throw until your right arm is fully extended above. Your left hand will be throwing a long toss up to a catch in your extended right hand. Your right hand will catch the ball and then let it roll off the finger tips, lifting it very slightly and directing it over and down to a catch in the left hand.

Work on getting your posture so you are erect, your right arm is fully extended, and your left hand is catching close to the left side of your body just above waist level, just like the Statue of Liberty!

ONE HANDED TRICKS

Two In One Hand

Two in one hand is easy. It is a very important basic move that will come in handy in learning many three ball variations, especially the through the pattern tricks. It is also most important in learning to juggle four balls as the basic four ball pattern is not a cascade, but juggling two balls in independent patterns in each hand.

You should learn to juggle two balls in one hand in three different basic patterns.... *outward, inward,* and *in place.*

Juggling two balls in one hand, in an outward pattern is called a
"Fountain.". An inward pattern is an *"Inward Fountain.".* When
the balls don't circulate and just move up and down in their own individual columns, this is called *"In Place".*

Two Ball Fountain

Start with two balls in the right hand. Throw the first ball up
about twelve inches and slightly to the right so that it can be caught
about six inches to the right of the throwing point. The second ball
follows the same line so that the two balls circulate through this line
in an outward direction on the right side of your body. Try not to turn
inward. If you are turning inward to keep the pattern going, press
each throw farther to the right so you have to reach to the right to
catch it. If turning is still a problem for you, open a door and stand so
the edge of the door is against your chest. Extend your arm and start
the outward fountain. The door will keep you from turning inward.
Reverse this instruction to work on your left hand.

Two Ball Inward Fountain

The inward fountain works just the opposite. Throw the first
right hand ball up to about twelve inches, hooking the throw slightly
inward so that the ball is caught about six inches to the left of the
throwing point. The two balls will circulate inward along this line. Try
not to turn! Don't forget to use the door if you need it. Reverse the
instruction for your left hand.

Two In Place

Throw the first right hand throw straight up. The second throw
goes straight up next to it. Reach back and forth to catch. Try to
keep your columns as vertical as possible.

Now that you know the basic two ball in one hand moves, exercise them by stretching the pattern higher, wider, and lower.
Combine them all into a routine like four throws fountain, four throws
in place, four throws inward fountain, then four more throws in place.

It is very important to develop your bad side as you work on your good side. Soon you will want to work with four and five balls. This will be very hard if you are not equally confident on both sides.

Three in One Hand

Juggling three balls in one hand is very difficult, but learning it will greatly increase your hand speed and greatly improve your three ball tricks. It will no doubt take you many weeks to get good control of three balls in one hand.

Start out with three balls in the right hand. Throw each ball outward to create a fountain pattern. Throw each ball to a height of about two feet above your head. Make sure each ball travels the same line, reaches the same height, and lands about eight inches to the right of the throwing point. Try just three throws at first, then go for more. Don't forget to work on your left hand too. Proper development of the left hand will be very important to you later on when you want to work on four and five balls.

Next, try it in columns. This is the pattern I prefer. The throwing order will be: right column, middle column, left column. Throw the balls about two feet above your head. Let your hand alternate between columns, right, middle, left, right, middle, left, and so on. Make sure you throw each ball to the same height and make sure each ball goes straight up in it's column. Again, don't forget to work on your left hand. A common mistake is to move your hand toward the catch before you have totally completed the previous throw. Finish releasing each throw, making sure it goes straight up before moving to make the next catch.

Once you can get a couple of passes with three in one hand, start playing with the pattern. Throw higher, then low as you can. Make your fountain circle rounder, then try the inward fountain. Spread your columns as far apart and as high as possible, then in close and low.

Three in One Hand - Multiplex

Three in one hand multiplex is actually the same as two in one hand except that one of the throws is a multiplex throw of two balls.

Start with three balls in the right hand. Throw the first ball normally, then the second two balls are thrown together multiplex. The first ball is caught normally and thrown back up, then the two balls are caught multiplex, and thrown back up multiplex to continue the cycle. This can be done in either the fountain pattern, inward fountain pattern, or in two columns.

Now start three in one hand either in a fountain or columns. Skip one throw and collect two balls to get into three in one hand multiplex. The real challenge is to get back into three in one hand. To do this, throw your multiplex throw a bit higher than normal. As you let go of the multiplex throw, snatch down on the single descending ball, quickly throw it back up, then quickly snatch down on the bottom ball of the multiplex throw which is now descending and quickly throw it back up. This should even out the spacing between the balls enough to recover the pattern.

Three in One Hand - Shoulder Throws

If you have really good control of three in one hand as well as shoulder throws, you are ready for this trick. If you're not that far yet, come back to it later.

Start a fountain pattern with three in the right hand. Pick any ball and throw it quickly over your right shoulder and back into the pattern. The shoulder throw has to reach the same height as the rest of your throws in order for it to re-enter the pattern at the proper point. Practice random throws, then go for every other, two consecutive, and finally "solids".

Three in One Hand - Shoulder Throws - Multiplex

Try a multiplex throw over the shoulder with two balls a few times. You'll find that you have to really lift them to get them to separate as they pass over the shoulder.

Next start three in one hand multiplex. Columns is probably the easiest. Throw some random shoulder throws with the single ball, then try a few with the two multiplex balls. When you are comfortable go for shoulder "solids".

Three in One Hand - Left to Right and Back

Spend a lot of time on this one! If you ever want to learn five balls, it will be a great asset.

Start a three ball fountain on the right side, lets say for six throws. Throw the seventh, eighth, and ninth throws across to your left hand and recover the three ball fountain in the left hand. Make sure the throws across to the left all reach the same height. Try to make six throws with the left hand, then throw the three balls back to the right hand in the same manner so that you can recover the pattern in your right hand.

Next, try to keep the three balls circulating from right to left and back. Your throwing pattern will be right, right, right, left, left, left, right, right, right, left, left, left and so on. You will throw three consecutive right hand throws to the left hand, then make three consecutive left hand throws back to the right.

OVER HEAD TRICKS

Cascade Over Head

The over head cascade is quite easy. Start with two balls. Flex your knees and bend back so that your hands are palm up to the ceiling. Push the balls up in a normal cascade pattern. It may take you a few tries before you discover where "UP" really is. Practice the two ball cascade in this position until you have fair control, then start working on three. Start with short runs of just a few throws, then try to get to ten consecutive throws. Exercise the pattern by throwing higher and wider, then as low as possible. For extra practice, try an over head reverse cascade.

Next, try to get from a regular cascade up to an over head cascade. Start your regular cascade. Throw one ball high and slightly back over your head. Flex your knees and bend back, quickly raising your arms so your hands are palm up to the ceiling. Push the next throw up and under the descending ball to start the over head cascade.

To get out, push any throw high and slightly forward. Drop your arms and turn your hands over. The first throw goes under the descending ball to start the normal cascade.

Shower Over Head

Start out again with two balls, but both in the right hand. Flex the knees and bend back raising the arms so hands are palm up to the ceiling. Push the right hand throws up and over to be caught in the left hand to form the over head shower pattern. Exercise this a bit, then try for three balls. Start with one pass, then go for more throws. The over head shower will also work with a multiplex throw.

A great exercise for both the over head cascade and shower is to go directly from one move to the other and back. Try it! Also try to reverse the direction of the shower.

One Up - Two Up Over Head

The method is the same as was used for the over head shower and cascade. Push the first ball from the right up the center, then push the two balls up in columns on the right and the left. Each ball moves up and down in it's own column. If you look closely you will see that you are juggling two balls over head with the right hand and one in the left. Try this same trick starting with two balls in the left. This will make your left hand do all the work.

For a real challenge, combine these tricks into a routine. Start a normal cascade. Throw up to an over head cascade, then change to a shower, then one up-two up, back to an over head cascade, and back down to a normal cascade.

THROUGH THE PATTERN TRICKS

Two in Place - One Through - Back and Forth

This is an easy trick, but it takes a while to work out the coordination between your right and left hands.

Start a three ball cascade, then stop throwing from the left hand and go into two balls in the right hand in an outward fountain pattern. Throw each ball quite high at first. Take your left hand and get it close to the two ball pattern. What you want to do is pass your left arm through the pattern at the wrist. Start to count your throws, one, two, one, two. A split second after you throw number one, pass your left arm through the pattern until the ball touches the side of your right shoulder. Hold it there and continue throwing from the right hand counting one, two, one, two. Wait a few throws, then just after number one again, pass your arm back through the pattern and continue the two ball fountain.

Practice random passes through the pattern, then try for two consecutive passes, in and out, so that the arm passes through the pattern, then one throw is made, then the arm passes back through and out. Next try "solid" passes through the pattern. The throw and pass order goes like this: one, pass, two, pass, one, pass, two, pass, and so on. Practice this on both sides.

Two in Place - One Through - Round and Round

This is almost the same as the previous explanation except that when your first pass through the pattern reaches the side of your shoulder, take your hand up and over the top ball of the fountain in a circular motion and back to the starting point. Your arm only passes through the pattern from left to right, then circles up and over the ball and back to the starting point. Try making just one circle at first, then adjust the speed with which you make the circle so that your arm passes through the pattern just after each number one throw. The throw and pass order goes like this: one, pass, two, one, pass, two, one, pass, two, one, pass, two, and so on.

Ball on a String - Above

This is an easy one. Juggle two balls in the right hand in columns. You have to be able to maintain a very low pattern to make this trick look good. Watch the left ball. Bring your left hand close to the pattern with the ball showing clearly. With your left hand, start to mimic the up and down motion of the left ball so that your left hand is traveling up and down next to the left ball, going to the same height, next to and parallel to the left ball. Your left hand does nothing but move up and down next to the left ball.

Once you get the idea of what has to happen, start to move your left hand up and about eight inches above the left ball. Coordinate the up and down movement of your left hand so that it remains directly above the left, lower ball. It should travel up and down maintaining a constant eight inch separation from the ball below, so it looks like the left ball of the juggle and the ball in your left hand are connected by a string. Hold the ball in your left hand by your finger tips so that it really shows to the audience.

Try varying the height that you throw the left ball, and likewise vary the height that you lift the ball in your left hand so as to maintain the position above as well as the eight inch distance between the balls. Throw a few very low throws, then one high one, lifting the left hand pulling the bottom ball way up on the string, then follow with more low throws.

Ball on a String - Below

This is the same move as the ball on the string above, only you switch your left hand holding the ball so that it is below the left ball that is juggling in the right hand. The idea here is to make it look as though the bottom ball held in your left hand is pushing up the ball above it on an invisible rod. Again, keep the ball in your left hand directly below the left ball being juggled and maintain the distance between them at about eight inches. Change the height of the left throw occasionally to make the pattern more interesting.

The Fake On the Left

Start juggling two balls in columns in the right hand. With a ball in your left hand, mimic the up and down movement of the juggled ball in the right column. Match the height as close as possible and be sure to show the ball in the left hand clearly to the audience.

The Fake - Alternating Sides

You already know the fake on the left. Now learn the fake on the right, but with one of the balls a color ball. Start a two ball juggle in the left hand, in columns. Make your color ball stay in the right column of the left hand juggling pattern. With a ball in the right hand, mimic the up and down movement of the juggled ball in the left column. Your right hand is just showing a ball moving up and down in unison with the left column. What you want to do is toss the color ball back and forth from left hand to right while alternately tossing, then showing the two balls in the outer columns.

When you toss the color ball to your right hand, throw the right ball straight up and catch the color ball. Your left hand is free with a ball in it so raise it to mimic the motion of the ball that was thrown up in the right column. As the two outer balls come down, toss the color ball back to your left. Throw the ball that you were just showing in your left hand straight up, then catch the color ball. The ball in your right hand is doing nothing so raise it to mimic the motion of the ball in the left column. As the left ball comes down, throw the color ball back to the right, and so on.

The Fake Behind the Back

Here's an easy fake trick that was used by *W. C. Fields* . Besides being a famous comedic actor, Fields was a great juggler. Many of his films show him doing parts of his act.

Start the cascade then do a two ball outward fountain in the left hand. Turn to your left a bit, then tuck your right arm behind your back just enough so that the audience can't see the ball in your right hand. Lift your right arm up and down to the same tempo that your left hand is juggling so it appears that you are making behind the back throws with the right hand. As you do the fake throws, gradually bring your right arm out enough to show the audience that you're faking it. You can then look at the ball, without stopping the juggle in the left hand, breathe on it, and shine it on your shirt like an apple, then throw it back into the cascade.

Tick-Tock

Tick-tock is easy. Juggle two balls low, in columns, in the left hand. Take the ball in the right hand up in front of your forehead. By bending at the wrist, swing the ball back and forth like a pendulum above the two ball juggling pattern. When the left column ball is high, swing the pendulum to the right. When the right column ball is high, swing the pendulum to the left. This is a good trick to do in time with a piece of music. You can over-dub eight or ten "tick-tocks" on to the music to create a great effect.

Around The Head

Around the head is also very easy. Juggle two balls in an outward fountain in the left hand. Take the right hand, showing the ball in the finger tips, and circle it counter clockwise around your head. This is a good trick to combine with a through the pattern trick or tick-tock.

Wiping You're Brow

Start your cascade and get into your routine, working up to your most difficult tricks. You're pushing hard, juggling furiously, and really working up a sweat! Now go into a low, two ball fountain in the left hand. Raise your right arm slowly and wipe your brow with the back of the right hand showing obvious relief to have gotten through it all! Throw the ball back into a cascade and continue!

PIROUETTE TRICKS

One Up - Pirouette

If you have a good cascade, this should not be too difficult. First off, try a couple of pirouettes. I turn to my left, pushing off with my right foot and turning on my left foot. It's important that your body remains erect during the pirouette, and that you turn a full 360 degrees. As soon as you push off with your right foot, tuck it in close to your left leg and step out as soon as you complete one revolution. A pirouette properly done will allow you to step out of the turn in exactly the same place you started. If you have any dance training at all you may have learned to turn the other way on the other foot. If this is the case, by all means turn the way you are accustomed to. You will need to do a quick, snappy pirouette to be able to do this trick.

Start a three ball cascade. Get your right foot in the push off position. Throw one right hand very high and go for one pirouette. When you are three quarters of the way around the pirouette, start looking up for the ball. If you threw the ball straight up and didn't travel too much during the pirouette, it should be easy to recover the cascade. The two most common faults are an inaccurate vertical throw and traveling on the pirouette. Many people start to turn before the ball is completely released. Make sure that you have completely released the ball before you do the turn.

Two Up - Pirouette

If your one up-pirouette went well, you should have no trouble with two up. There are two ways to throw up the two balls, columns, and crossing like a cascade. I prefer columns only because during the typical three ball routine, the balls are cascading a great deal of the time, so it's nice to see columns for a change. Your pirouette will have to be even snappier for this one. Also, your throws must be very accurate.

Start the cascade and get your right foot ready for the push off. Take any right and throw it high, straight up in a column on your right. Quickly take the next right and throw it high in the column inside and next to the first high throw. Spin like crazy! As you come around, look for the ball coming down in the right column, (you could make this a color ball), catch it and watch for the next ball coming down now in the middle, then recover the cascade.

If you are having trouble catching the first ball, examine the accuracy of that throw and the speed of your pirouette. Make sure you're not traveling on the pirouette. If you are getting the first ball all right and missing the second, try throwing the second throw slightly higher than the first. This will give you a split second more time in which to recover the cascade.

If you want to try two up-pirouette with the high throws crossing, the mechanics of the situation are the same, except that the two high throws are a right and a left instead of right, right. Also, when you finish the pirouette you have to look to your left to catch the first descending ball. You can also throw left, right, then look for the first ball on your right. Take your pick or try them all!

If you make the color ball the first high throw, it will be the one to look for when you come out of the pirouette.

Three Up - Pirouette

This is a tough one. You have to throw very accurately and spin very fast to make it. Try it in columns first, throwing the right straight up in the right column, the left straight up in the left column, and the next right straight up the middle.

There is a technique that comes in handy when you want to throw a lot of objects into the air at one time and have enough time left to do something before they come back down. It's called *compressing the pattern*.

The concept is quite difficult to convey in print, but say you cascade three balls at a constant tempo. If you make three consecutive high throws at the same tempo, unless you've thrown the balls extremely high, the first high throw will have probably hit the ground before you've even had the chance to start a pirouette. Since the first ball you throw high will be coming down first, you must throw the second and third balls fast enough, and pirouette fast enough, to get around before the first ball descends past the catching point. The less time that passes between the first throw and the pirouette, the better off you'll be. It's easy to delay the first throw to shorten this period. By delaying the first throw, you will push the second and third throws closer together, thus compressing the pattern. I'll try to give you a better picture.

I'll name the throws for you. Figure that the word "and" represents the time between the throws. Start the cascade, then the typical set up for three up-pirouette would be:

r i g h t, a n d, l e f t, a n d, r i g h t, a n d, l e f t........... a...n...d,

right, loft, right, pirouctto, and recover.

Of course it is most important that the throws be accurate and the pirouette be very quick. Make sure all three high throws go at least to the same height. You can make the pattern recovery a bit easier if you push the second and third high throws progressively higher so that they come down a split second later.

If you do the three up using columns, look to your right for the first ball to catch after the pirouette. If you want to try a cascade, you still throw right, left, right, but crossing. Look to the left after the pirouette. You could also throw left, right, left, crossing, pirouette, and then look to your right for the first ball. Remember, if you make the color ball your first high throw, it will be easy to pick out as the first ball to catch after the pirouette.

The Half Turn Throwing One

Before you start to juggle, first learn the half turn, turning to your left. Lift your left heel and "plant" your left toe on the ground slightly behind you. You will use your left toe to pull yourself around.

Turn to your left, push off with your right foot and pull with your left toe so that you make a complete about face.

Practice this a few times, then start the cascade. Plant your left toe and get ready to make the about face. Pick any right hand ball, throw it high so that it travels back over the middle of your head and comes down slightly behind you. As you release the ball, turn quickly, all the way around. Keep your eye on the high ball. You should be able to see it go up and over as you turn, then recover the cascade by starting with the right hand. Practice random half turns, then try throwing the color ball high each time it comes to first your right, and then your left hand.

The tendency is to throw the ball too far behind you so that you have to step forward to catch it. Adjust the angle of the high throw so that it comes comfortably down to your right hand after the half turn.

The Half Turn Throwing Three

This will be quite difficult, maybe even more so than three up-pirouette. Start the cascade using the color ball, and then plant your foot. Starting with the color ball from the right, throw three consecutive crossing throws back over your head. Compress the pattern just as you would for three up-pirouette and throw in a high, narrow pattern. Quickly make the half turn, watching the color ball all the way up and over. Catch the color ball first, in the right hand, then just watch the other balls go by. Do this a few times adjusting the throw of the first, color ball until it can be caught comfortably after the turn, then concentrate on cleaning up the throw of the second ball so it too can be caught as easily as the first. The same goes for the third ball.

Don't forget to compress the pattern to give you time to make the turn. If you are having trouble getting around for the first ball, compress more, throw all three balls higher, and if necessary, push the second and third throws progressively higher to give you more time.

It's a good idea to count the three throws and the three catches, one, two, three....one, two, three. This way if you are having trouble with catch number two, it's because throw number two is bad. Adjust the angle of each throw so that they all come down behind you within comfortable reach.

Half Turn - One Up - Two Up

If you can already do the half turn with three balls crossing, one up - two up should be no problem.

Start a cascade then get into one up - two up. Begin by throwing just the single ball back over your head, do the half turn and continue the one up - two up pattern. Next, throw the two balls in unison up and behind you, turn and recover the pattern. Last, throw the single ball, then the two balls in unison, turn and recover.

Three Ball Take Aways or "Steals"

If you are lucky enough to have a friend who is also learning how to juggle, you can try these tricks together.

Start your cascade using the color ball. Have your friend get very close to your left side and watch the color ball cycle through the pattern. Your friend should lift up his or her right hand and slide it half way across your chest, being careful not to disturb your juggle. As you throw the color ball from your left to right hand, your friend should beat you to the catch, grabbing it with a right, while at the same time stepping in front of you. You continue with your next two throws which are also "stolen" in order by your friend. As you step away and behind, your friend should now be cascading the three balls. Line yourself up next to your friend now and "steal" them back! With practice, you and your friend can go around and around very fast so that you each throw only three throws before the other "steals" them away.

Front Take Aways

Front take aways are easy. Stand facing your partner as he or she cascades three balls. Watch the color ball cycle through the pattern, then quickly, one, two, three, beat your partner to the catch and snatch the three balls away without stopping the cascade.

Take Aways from Behind and Over Head

Have your partner crouch down and begin a chest high three ball cascade. Go behind and look down over your partners shoulders. The pattern should look familiar from this view point so reach over and take it away. If you lift one of your legs, your partner can slip through, then you crouch down and let your partner "steal" the pattern from you.

Three Ball Drop Backs

If both you and your partner have a good solid cascade, the drop back should be no problem. Start your cascade and have your partner stand about three feet directly behind you. Starting with the right, throw three consecutive crossing throws back, up and over your head so that your partner can catch them in order and continue the cascade. Your throws must be very even and come down within catching reach of your partner so that he or she can comfortably catch the first two throws and then start the cascade when the third one arrives. You can help your partner out by throwing the third ball a bit higher than the rest. Practice for a bit with just two balls so you can scope out the correct throwing angle and distance. Once you have it, you and your partner can keep changing places by doing drop backs again and again.

BEHIND THE BACK TRICKS

Back Crosses

Start with one ball in the right hand. Practice throwing it around behind the back so that it comes up and over your left shoulder, about ear height and about ten inches from your ear. The ball should peak just above your ear, then fall to a comfortable catch in the left hand. Don't twist your body or dip your left shoulder. Stand up straight and square, make your wrist and arm do the work. Try the left hand throw also, then practice throwing left and right back crosses with one ball until you have good control. Try some higher and lower throws to improve your control.

Next, take one ball in each hand and try the double back cross. Throw first from the right, then left, catch left, catch right, and stop. Repeat this exercise and adjust your throws so that you can catch on both sides comfortably. Remember to stand straight and square, don't dip your shoulders,

Now, start the three ball cascade. Pick any right and throw it to a back cross. Repeat this a few times to get the feel of it, then try this. Start your cascade pattern and move the entire pattern toward the right side of your body. It will be easier to get a right throw out of the pattern and into the back cross throw. Practice random right and left back cross throws, then try throwing a back cross with the color ball each time it comes to your right and left hand.

"Solids" back crosses are quite difficult, so start by throwing two consecutive throws, right, left, and recover. Also try left, right, and recover, then gradually add throws until you can do ten consecutive back crosses.

Behind the Back and Under the Arm

Do a couple of back crosses with one ball throwing from the right hand. Notice that the ball comes over the shoulder. Now, make the same back cross reaching around your back a little farther than normal. Before you release the ball, lift your left arm up and back so that the ball goes under your left arm instead of over your left shoulder. It helps if you arch your back and shift your weight to your heels. With practice you will be able to do every other ball and even "solids".

Shoulder Throws

Shoulder throws are similar to back crosses except that instead of passing behind the back, they pass over the same shoulder as the hand they are thrown from.

Take one ball in the right hand. Throw it over your right shoulder so that it passes by the right side of your head at the right temple, and lands in the left hand. This is quite an unnatural motion, so don't worry if it doesn't come easy for you. Again, don't drop your shoulders or twist your body to make the throw easier. Make your arm and wrist do the work.

Practice throwing one ball back and forth from left to right, then get the second ball and try the right, left, stop, and the left, right, stop.

Finally, start the three ball cascade, then throw random shoulder throws until you have good control, then go for two consecutive throws. Next, throw the color ball each time it arrives left and right, then go for "solids", starting with three consecutive throws and increasing as your ability allows.

BOUNCE TRICKS

Many bounce tricks are not difficult to do and can be quite valuable when constructing an interesting routine. However, ball bouncing of large numbers in intricate patterns can be extremely difficult requiring years of practice and precision timing. There are many good ball bouncers, but I don't think that in the world today there is one better than *Paul Bachman*!

Forced Bounce Cascade

A forced bounce is when you throw a ball down with enough force to make it bounce back up to at least the same height it was thrown from.

Find a good solid floor and get two pieces of opaque tape. Mark a spot in the middle of the floor. Put down two pieces of tape about six inches apart. These will be your bouncing points. Start with two balls in the right and one in the left, both hands palm up. Spread your feet about two feet apart and position yourself so that when you look down you are looking directly at the two marks, one on the left and one on the right. Throw the first right ball down to the left mark. Throw it with enough force that it bounces just up to your left hand and catch. Take the same ball and throw it back from the left to the right mark, to bounce just up to the right and catch. Aim all of your right hand throws to the left mark, and your left hand throws to the right mark.

Now try to get the cascade going. Start with the right. The first ball goes down to the left mark, as it bounces up, throw the left ball *UNDER* it, and to the right mark. As the second ball bounces, the third ball is thrown *UNDER* it, to the left mark. The catches are made palm up. Each ball should bounce slightly higher than the point from which they are thrown so that they peak and land lightly in your palm up hands. Repeat this right, left, right cycle to get the feel of what is supposed to happen, then gradually add throws until you can make ten consecutive.

Toss Bounce Reverse Cascade

The toss bounce reverse cascade creates a very interesting bounce effect. The toss bounce technique will be quite valuable later on for bouncing large numbers of objects because of the degree with which you can slow the pattern down.

For the toss bounce, you will lightly toss each ball about chin high, let gravity take it to hit the floor, then bounce up to the opposite hand. The ball should just make it to the catching hand. The height of the toss depends on how good of a ball you are using, and how hard the floor is. A good silicone ball has almost total recovery, so on a good floor you only need to toss them up a few inches.

This will be an easy trick to learn so start with all three balls, two in the right hand, palms up for the throws. Get over your two marks. Toss the first right up to about chin height so it peaks and falls to the vicinity of the left mark. As it peaks at your chin, toss the second ball from the left up and *OVER* the first ball and past your chin to bounce at the right mark, catch left, catch right, and stop. Try this a few times to get the feel of the toss, then go for three throws.

The important thing is that you toss each ball to the same chin height, with the same crossing angle, be sure that the balls pass *OVER* each other. Practice one, two, three, a few times then try for longer runs. Thus far you have probably been catching by letting the ball bounce up and into your hand, palm up. When you get "solids" going, you will need to turn your hand over and lightly snatch each ball palm down for the catch, then turn the hand over to toss again. Start with three throws, increasing gradually until you make ten consecutive.

It's easy to get from a regular cascade into the toss bounce reverse cascade. Start your regular cascade, then starting from the right, make three consecutive reverse cascade throws and don't catch them. All three will bounce, look to your left for the first ball. Turn your hands palm down to snatch catch. You are now into the toss bounce reverse cascade.

Forced Bounce Cascade - Through the Legs

Take one ball in the right hand. Lift the right leg slightly and hold it in front of you just enough so that you can throw the ball under it, just behind the knee, to a bounce near your marks and back up to your left hand. Now lift your left leg and do the same bouncing from left to right. Since you are throwing from a wider angle, you don't have to be too concerned with hitting the right or left mark in particular. If the balls bounce in the vicinity of the marks that will be good enough. Repeat the cycle with one ball until you are comfortable with the pattern, then move on.

Get three balls and start the forced bounce cascade using the color ball. When the color ball comes to your right hand, lift your right leg and go for the under the leg throw. Try to keep the pattern going, wait for the color ball to cycle back to your right hand, then go for it again. Actually, what you are ultimately trying to do is maintain the cascade bouncing pattern while moving your leg through the open spots. Practice throwing the color ball under the right leg, then try your left. Work toward throwing the color ball under the leg each time it comes to the right or left.

If you bounce every right hand throw under first the right leg, and then the left leg, you will find that you naturally turn in a circle to your left. A full revolution of this trick would be a great addition to your three ball routine. Your right throws alternate under the right and left legs. All of your catches go to a bounce.

Toss Bounce Reverse Cascade - Leg Overs

Begin your toss bounce reverse cascade. Notice that there are large gaps in the pattern between where you throw and where the ball bounces. Take a ball in the left hand. Toss bounce it toward your right side. When it's about half way to the floor, lift your right leg, bending at the knee, up and over the ball. When the ball bounces up, put your foot back on the floor and catch the ball in your right hand. Now throw it back to a bounce on the left, lifting the left leg up and over. Start your toss bounce reverse cascade and try random leg overs. Work up to the point where you do "solid" leg overs on both sides.

The Three Ball Drop

This is very easy. Begin your regular three ball cascade. Starting with any right, toss each ball lightly, straight up in columns, right, left, middle, and let them bounce one time each. Turn your hands over palm down to snatch catch right and left. Squat slightly. Let the third, middle ball bounce to its peak, then start with a normal throw from either hand to recover the regular cascade.

The Three Ball Drop - Pirouette

Another easy trick! Do the three ball drop as explained, except toss the balls just a bit higher in columns. As they are dropping toward the bounce, quickly pirouette, snatch catch right and left, squat, and recover the cascade. If you have a good quick pirouette, you will not have to toss the balls very high. If you are having any trouble recovering the cascade after the drop, try tossing the third, middle ball higher than all the rest. It will bounce later and higher, giving you time to snatch catch left and right and then look for the last ball.

If you happen to be more athletic, possibly a gymnast, you can put a back handspring, back flip, or some other short acrobatic in place of the pirouette. If you need more time, compress the pattern and throw higher, or let the balls bounce twice.

Continuous Drops With One Hand

Do the three ball drop as explained. With the right hand only, snatch catch and toss each ball as it peaks in it's column. Toss so that each ball remains in it's column and your right hand circulates through the columns right, left middle, right, left, middle, right, left, middle. If you want to slow the pattern down, toss each ball higher. Remember to keep the balls in their columns.

The Forced Bounce Shower

This works the same as a regular shower, except it's upside down. Go to your marks on the floor and remove one of them. Spread your legs about two feet apart, and position yourself over the mark so that when you bend your head over, you are looking straight down at the mark. Start with two balls in the right and one in the left, then just as you would with a regular shower, throw the two balls in the right, down to bounce at your mark. Throw right, right, then pass off the left ball to the right hand and throw right again. Every right throw from there on goes to a forced bounce on the mark. Every catch will be a left, palm down snatch catch which is passed off to the right.

The Shower Through the Legs

Spread your feet to a distance of about two feet with your body centered over the floor marks. Twist your torso to the right so your right leg is forward and your left leg is back. With two balls in your right hand and one in your left, start the shower so that the balls bounce off the marks, under your torso, and back up to your left hand. Make the pass off in front of your body, then make the right throw to the floor again.

The Floor Roll Shower

Take all three balls in the right hand. Kneel down and place the right hand on the floor palm up with fingers pointing to the left. Let the balls roll out of your hand one at a time so that they roll about one foot across to your left hand. Pick up each ball as it comes, hand it back to your right hand, then let it roll out again towards the left hand. Control the roll of each ball to maintain even spacing between the three balls. To slow the pattern down even more, move your hands farther apart.

The Cascade Off the Wall

This is just like a cascade in the air except that the balls will bounce at an angle off two spots on the wall. If you want, make two marks on the wall at about eye level and about eight inches apart. Right throws go to the left mark and left throws to the right mark. Start out close to the wall, then move farther away while continuing the cascade. Try going from a regular cascade to a wall bounce and then back to the regular cascade.

The Shower Off the Wall

Mark one spot on the wall at eye level. Every right throw will go to that mark, bounce, then be caught in the left hand. The left hand passes off to the right, and so on. Try going from a regular shower to a wall shower and back. Also try going from a regular cascade to a wall shower and back to a regular cascade.

The Cascade and Shower Off Wall Behind You.

Stand with your back against the wall. Start a regular cascade, then throw each ball, both right and left, above and behind you, as if you were going to do the three ball half turn. The balls will bounce off of two points above your shoulders, then down to your hands. You can also shower the balls by throwing each right to a point directly above your head. They will bounce off and down to your left hand. Pass each ball to your right and throw again. Try various combinations of regular cascade, to wall bounce, to shower wall bounce, to regular cascade, turn around to cascade off wall behind, to shower off wall behind, and back to the regular cascade.

Bouncing Off a Drum

A great effect for a professional routine is bouncing balls off a drum. *Bobby May* used a drum in his act for nearly his entire career. *Rudy Horn* is famous for bouncing seven balls off a drum with incredible ease. *Paul Bachman* also uses a drum to great advantage, in fact, his drum was given to him by *Bobby May*. Find a used drum and get a heavy duty head for it. Make four short legs with the two closest being a few inches shorter than the back legs. This will tilt the drum head towards you. Stand a fair distance away and throw the balls at the drum head. Adjust your distance until the throw angle makes the balls return to the proper catching point. On certain surfaces, rubber feet should keep the drum in place, but sometimes you will need to have some type of adapter that you can slip on the leg tips so you can add pointed feet that will dig in better. You can either tune the hollow drum or use the snares. Choose a piece of music that you can keep the beat with, preferably something that is popularly associated with a drum beat like "Yankee Doodle".

Bouncing From Floor to Wall

You can combine the floor and wall bounce like this. Get a few feet away from a wall. Bounce each ball off the floor at an angle so that the balls ricochet off the wall and back to the catching point or reverse it and toss or throw the balls at the wall first so they ricochet off the floor and back to the catch.

Foot Trap to Over the Shoulder Heel Kick

This trick is best learned with a sponge ball or a tennis ball.

First learn the foot trap. Take one ball and drop it towards your right toe. Just before the ball hits your toe, lift your right foot up and pivot it to the right. As the ball passes, quickly cover the ball and trap it on the floor under your right toe. You have to time your right foot so that you trap the ball at the exact moment it hits the floor. The ball should not bounce at all. Work on this with one ball, then go back to your lacrosse balls and try the toss to the foot trap on a throw right out of the cascade.

Next, learn the heel kick. Go back to the sponge or tennis ball. Place the ball between your heels so it touches the floor. Squeeze your heels together lightly, just enough to hold the ball snug. Jump up and forward, kicking your heels so as to throw the ball up and over your right shoulder. Be sure to jump up. Don't just kick! As you finish the kick, look to your right to catch the ball. It may take you some time to get the feel of this. If you try it every time you drop a ball instead of just picking it up, you will get it in no time at all. You will have to twist your legs a bit to the right on the kick to get the ball up and over your right shoulder.

Now put the two together. Drop a ball out of the cascade to a foot trap. Roll your right foot off the ball to your right, then make a small jump forward to get the ball between your heels. With practice you should be able to make the transition from foot trap to heels very quickly. Kick the ball from the heels, up and over the right shoulder, and recover the cascade by starting with the right hand.

Leg Overs

Start the regular cascade. Throw one ball up the middle to about eye level. Just before the ball hits the floor, lift your right leg up, over the ball, and back to the floor, then recover the cascade. Lift up and over fast enough so that by the time the ball bounces back up, your leg is out of the way. Work on this with both legs, then try getting the right and left over on a double bounce of the ball. Throw the ball a bit higher, let it bounce, right leg over, let it bounce again, left leg over, then recover.

Jump Overs

This is the same as leg overs except that you jump all the way over the ball using a scissors jump. Toss a ball to about eye level. Start to jump at your first chance to get the right leg over the ball. As your right leg goes over, push off with your left leg, lifting it up and over the ball. For a moment, both feet are in the air at the same time. Land on the right side of the ball, then recover the cascade. Practice your scissors jump so that your left leg follows quickly behind your right. When you get the scissors jump right, try this. Toss a ball to a bounce, leg over, let it bounce again, jump over, and recover. If you learn the scissors jump leading with both left and right, try tossing a ball to a bounce, jump over from right to left, let it bounce again, then jump over from left to right, and recover.

BODY BOUNCE TRICKS

The Knee Bounce

The knee bounce is very easy. Make a very short toss with a ball, about chest high. Raise the right or left leg so that the thigh is parallel to the ground, meeting the falling ball at the parallel point. The ball should hit on the meaty part of your leg, just above the knee. Give the ball a soft, but firm strike when it hits the knee. With constant repetition you will develop consistent control. Work on a toss to each knee, then try a toss to the right knee, bounce from the right to the left and back. Next work on multiple bounces on one knee, then combinations of all of those. A good routine to try with one ball is: right knee, left knee, right knee, to floor bounce leg over, to right knee, to floor bounce, jump over, and stop.

The Knee To Foot Bounce

Hold the ball above the knee. Drop it bringing the knee up to meet it only part way. Let the ball hit the knee. Don't strike it with the knee. The ball should bounce off the knee and be heading for the floor in front of you. As the ball bounces off your knee, straighten your lower leg and flick your foot to kick the ball back up to your hand. The ball should strike your foot right on the joint where your toes meet your foot. Having a good flat shoe helps on this one.

This is a good trick to throw out of the cascade. The ball hits knee, foot, then is kicked back up and into the cascade. If you want a real challenge, try knee, foot, knee, foot, knee, foot, without touching the ball after the initial drop!

Foot Bounces

Here's three ways to throw a ball out of the cascade and then bounce or kick it back up into the pattern from various points of the foot. These are the type of bounces that you see the guys doing with a hacky sack. I am sure your kicks will be very erratic for a while, so be sure to practice these in an area far away from breakables.

Start a cascade, then toss one ball out in front on almost a straight line toward the floor so if allowed to continue it will hit the floor about five feet in front of you. As the ball heads toward the floor, lift your right leg, bending at the knee. Straighten the knee and smack the ball with your foot so that the strike is made with the flat part of your foot just behind the toe joint. The timing of this move is quite difficult to master so to save your foot it might be a good idea to use a tennis or sponge ball for a while.

Next, start a cascade. Toss a right hand throw up in a column about twelve inches to your right. As the ball heads for the floor, kick the ball straight up using the outside of the foot. Practice this on both sides, then try to kick the ball all the way from the right foot to the left foot, then kick up from the left foot back into the cascade. Also work on multiple bounces on each part of the foot followed by a kick back into the pattern.

Next, after starting the cascade, toss one ball up the middle column. Before it hits the floor, kick it with the inside of your foot back up into the pattern. Work on your left foot, then go for a right inside kick to a left inside kick and back into the pattern.

If you really work on the body bounces, kicks, and neck catches, you can put together long routines. Here are some combinations that you can work on. Try to get all the way through each routine, then recover the cascade. When you see a "start" mentioned, look in the "Starts" section for a description.

1. Knee bounce to outside of foot kick.

2. Between the heels kick start to knee bounce.

3. Knee bounce to inside foot kick to outside foot kick.

4. Right outside kick to right inside kick to left inside kick to left outside kick and back to the pattern.

5. Between the heels kick start to knee bounce to neck catch to head bounce to floor bounce leg over to jump over and back to pattern.

6. Three over shoulder start to neck catch to neck throw to head bounce to right knee bounce to left knee bounce to right knee bounce to floor bounce to right knee bounce and back to pattern.

The Forearm and Back of Hand Bounce

There are three good places on your arm that you can do controlled bounces. The back of the hand, the inside of the forearm with the arm outstretched and palm up, and the back of the forearm with the arm bent back hand by the ear.

Practice bouncing one ball off of these points, then try bouncing a random ball from the regular cascade off any one point. Try Multiple bounces off the inside of the forearm, and then work towards bouncing every ball that is thrown from the left hand to first the back of hand, then inside forearm, then back of forearm, alternating in that order. Learn this alternating order for three passes, then go to five consecutive bounces on the inside of the forearm, then back into the cascade.

The Hand To Bicep Bounce

Take a ball in your left hand. Toss is to your right hand so that it hits your right palm at about the heel of your hand with your right arm bent slightly. Let the ball hit the heel of your right hand so that it ricochets back toward your bicep. As it ricochets, straighten your arm so that the ball strikes your bicep and rebounds to your left hand. Try this right out of a cascade. You have to be quick to make the hand bicep bounce and still recover the pattern. *W. C. Fields* did this trick "solids" on both sides!

The Chest Roll

The chest roll is not really a toss juggling move. It involves rolling a ball from the back of the right hand, all the way along your right arm, across your chest, all the way along your left arm, and into your left hand.

Start with your right arm outstretched, slightly bent at the elbow, and palm out. Take the ball with your left hand and place it on the back of your right hand. With a sharp snap of the left hand, make the ball roll along the inside, top of your arm, toward your chest. As the ball gets to your right elbow, straighten your arm and contract your chest to push the ball along its way. As the ball passes over your chest, contract your left shoulder so when the ball arrives, you can flex forward and push the ball up your left arm. Some females might have trouble with this for obvious reasons.

This flexing motion can only be learned with constant repetition. There is a fine touch to it. Keep practicing so that you get the ball to go farther each time. It might be a good idea to start learning this trick with a larger ball, perhaps a basketball, volleyball, or a soccer ball. Then, maybe work down to a soft ball, and then a juggling ball. When you get it, try throwing a ball from the cascade to a catch-on-the-roll on the back of the right hand, roll all the way around to be boosted off the left forearm, and back to recover the cascade. *Mark Nizer* is a master of this trick!

TRICKS USING THE HEAD

Shower Place Rolls

You have already learned some of the place roll tricks back in the cascade section. Try showering three balls throwing from the right hand. Snatch up one of the balls coming from the left hand and place it on the crown of your head. Now, leave the right hand up in the vicinity of your forehead. Instead of handing off the rest of the balls coming from the left hand, toss them up to the right hand. Snatch down with the right hand to catch each ball, lifting it quickly to placement on the crown of your head. Each ball should roll slowly off the left side of your head to a catch in the left hand. Every ball that comes to the right hand is placed on the head. Every throw from the left hand is tossed *UP* to the right hand. The better your placement is, the longer it will take for the ball to roll off. This will slow the action down considerably so be sure to pay extra attention to where you place the balls.

The Under The Chin Catch

This trick isn't one of my personal favorites, so I don't do it. I have seen a lot of other jugglers do it though, and I must admit it looks great and always gets good audience response.

Start a cascade. Use soft bean bags or light tennis balls at first. Pick any right hand throw and, quickly, but very *GENTLY*, place it up, and trap it under your chin. As you throw your next left throw, lift your chin to let the ball out, catch it left, and continue the cascade. Work up to the point that you can put every right hand throw *GENTLY* under the chin and then work on picking up speed.

The jugglers I have seen do this trick give the impression that they are really smacking the ball hard into their throat, complete with vocalized sound effects, thus the great audience response. They are acting! Don't do this trick unless you can do it *GENTLY !!!* Place the ball up and under your chin, *NOT* into your throat!

Toss to a Side Chin Catch

This one is similar to the under the chin catch except that you toss the ball to the opposite side of your chin to be caught between the side of your chin and your collar bone. Throw from the right hand to the right collar bone and from the left hand to the left collar bone. Hold the ball briefly after the catch, then drop it straight down to the appropriate hand to continue the cascade. To do "solids" throw every ball from both hands to a side of the chin catch. As each ball drops from the catch, the next throw goes to a catch on the other side of the chin.

The Head Bounce

The head bounce is a good, easy transition trick. Try a few bounces just with one ball. A sponge ball or tennis ball is good to learn with as it will take a great many bounces to get good control. Toss the ball up about twelve inches above your head. Look at it until the last second, then tip your head down slightly for the bounce, then quickly look back up. The ball should hit just above your hair line, not on the crown of your head. Bump the ball up slightly so it rebounds back to about the same point twelve inches above your head, and lands comfortably back in your hand.

Next, try multiple bounces. Start with two consecutive bounces. You will have to direct the first bounce straight up so that it comes back down on your head, and then direct the second bounce back to your hand.

Try to get up to five or more consecutive bounces, then try it out of the cascade. Start the cascade. Pick any right hand throw. Toss it up to a head bounce and direct the rebound so that it goes to your left hand, then recover the cascade. Try throwing from the left hand and bounce the ball to the right hand, and recover. Last, try bouncing every throw, both left and right, off the head. over to the opposite hand, and back into the pattern.

NECK CATCH TRICKS

The Neck Catch

The neck catch is the perfect trick to combine with head bounce, pirouette, and body bounce tricks.

Use a soft ball for the first few days. A sponge rubber ball is probably best because it has some weight to it. A bean bag or stuffed tennis ball will also do. Put on a tee shirt or sweat shirt, anything without a collar.

Get in a clear area, away from all furniture. Toss the ball about three feet over head. Focus on the descending ball until it is about a foot above you, then quickly bend forward and down so that the ball lands on the nape of your neck. As the ball lands, lift your chin and hunch your shoulders so that you make a pocket to hold the ball. You have to bend forward almost as fast as the ball is falling in order to break it's fall without the ball bouncing off your neck or the back of your head. If the ball bounces off, you are either bending too slow, or starting to bend too early. As you practice, adjust your timing so that the ball lands softly on the nape of your neck. Sometimes the ball will strike the back of your head before going to the neck. If this is the case, try tipping your head forward a little, right after you start bending for the catch. Just as the ball hits, pick your head back up and hunch your shoulders back.

The Neck Throw

Make a neck catch. Bend down a little so that the ball leans against the base of your skull. Bend far enough forward so that if you were to drop your chin the ball would roll up and over the top of your head. Now drop your head and as the ball starts rolling, quickly stand up straight, snapping your head back as the ball reaches the crown. This snapping action, if done with the proper timing, can shoot the ball high above you. You can then either re-catch it on your neck, do a head bounce, or start the cascade again. Practice this a few times, then quit until the next day. If you over do it, you will wake up with a very sore neck. If the ball is going behind you, you are snapping too soon. If it doesn't go up in the air, you are probably not bending your head down far enough to start the ball rolling toward the snap. If the ball rolls off of your head and goes straight to the floor, you are snapping too late. Work on the neck throw for short periods each day. You should begin to build stamina and see progress within one week.

Here's a short routine you can try using the neck catch and a few other tricks that you've already learned. Start a cascade. Do a half shower, then double shower, then one head bounce into a shower. Next do a head bounce, to a neck catch, to a head bounce, and back to the cascade.

ENGLISH OR EFFECT TRICKS

English or effect tricks are very useful when you have a good solid floor to work on. Dog balls or lacrosse balls work well for this, however, silicone balls are by far the best because they bounce so well. It is important to work on English tricks on a clean, hard floor. Linoleum over concrete is great. Keep a wet cloth around to wipe the balls with from time to time. You will need to have a good grip on the ball to get it to spin. It will also take some time to develop the hand muscles that you will be using on the English tricks so be patient.

The Front Hand Slap

The easiest English trick is probably the front hand slap. You will need lots of room to do this so get into an open area away from breakables. Take one ball and toss it about chin high in front of you. Take your hand and slap down hard at the ball, keeping the palm vertical. You want to put enough back spin and downward force on the ball to make it bounce hard about two feet in front of you, back up and over your head, bounce again behind you, and have enough rebound force and spin to return back over your shoulder and into your hand. At first you may have to kneel down so that the ball can return over your shoulder, but with practice you will be able to get it to come all the way back.

The Foot Slap

The foot slap will always come in handy when you have an unexpected drop. It works the same as the hand slap. You want to add downward force and back spin to the ball. Drop a ball from waist high. Let it bounce once or twice. Lift your foot with the toe tipped up as much as possible and slap down at the ball as it reaches it's peak after the bounce. You want to hit it hard enough and back spin it fast enough to make it bounce back up above waist level so you can easily recover your cascade.

The Side Cut

For the side cut, toss a ball chin high. With a flat, right hand, "karate" chop the right side of the ball to add downward force and side spin to the ball so that it bounces first to your left, then over to your right, then back to you.

The Two Ball Center Cut

Take two balls in one hand so they are sitting side by side in your hand. Toss them up a few inches so that they stay side by side and very close together. Take your flat, right hand and "karate" chop down hard between the two balls. The balls should separate both spinning inward, hit the floor about three feet apart, then rebound back to about the position you started from.

Thumb Snap Back Spins

Thumb snap back spins are probably the most controlable of all the back spin variations. Both *Bobby May* and *El Gran Picaso* used them in their three ball routines.

Put a ball in your hand, palm up. Using your thumb, squeeze the ball hard against your palm. Drop your arm down to your side, then toss the ball hard, up to head high, and away from you so that it lands about four feet in front of you. As you release the ball, snap your hand and thumb down hard to create back spin on the ball. It will probably take a few weeks to develop the muscles in the hand and wrist that will let you put an enormous amount of back spin on the ball. A throw that lands four feet in front of you should rebound all the way back to the throwing position.

Work on this with both hands, then you can do a three ball English bounce cascade off the floor, and then go back into the regular cascade pattern. To do this, throw your right throws to bounce four feet in front of you and to the left so they bounce back to your left hand. Throw the left throws over the rights so they bounce four feet in front of you on the right and back to your right hand. Continuous throws like this will result in an English bounce cascade.

Snaps to the Opposite Side

This is the English trick that I use most in my act. It's a combination of a wrist snap and a finger snap which creates a tremendous amount of side spin.

Squeeze a ball between the thumb tip and the tips of the first and second fingers. Squeeze hard, then bend the wrist down and twist the hand to your right. Quickly snap the wrist up and as you release the ball, squeeze and snap your fingers hard to create the side spin. The ball should travel up about one foot above your head and land about four feet to your left. The side spin should make it rebound at least as far back as to catch in your left hand. The snapping motion of your fingers is just like normally snapping your fingers. Again, it will take some time to develop the muscles necessary to do this trick well.

Work hard on both hands, then try a shower bounce to the left. Each throw from the right is a snap throw across to the left with each ball rebounding back to a catch in the left, then handed off to the right to be snap thrown across to the left again. Next, try a snap throw cascade. Throw right throws so they snap across left and rebound to the left hand. The left throws are snapped across to the right so they rebound the right. If you have good left and right side snaps, this cascade pattern is quite ease to sustain.

The Snap Neck Throw

Bobby May did this trick better than any one! If you look at his old films, you will see him do this great trick.

Throw a ball to a neck catch. Instead of snapping the ball up so it lands in front of you, straighten up early, so that it lands about three feet behind you. Dip your head extra far, snap your neck and straighten up extra hard, so that you create as much back spin as possible on the ball. The ball needs to go high enough so that it can rebound over your right or left shoulder and back into your cascade pattern.

English Ricochets

This is another *Paul Bachman* special! Take a ball in your right hand. Throw it down hard so that it hits the floor about three inches from the side of your right foot and bounces in to hit the outside of your right leg about six inches above your ankle. The harder you throw the ball, the more back spin you will create. The ball will ricochet off your ankle, bounce about four feet away from you, and rebound back to your right hand. *Bachman* does a pirouette while the ball is rebounding. *Rob Murray* used the ricochet in a different way. He had a vertical panel set off to his left. He would throw one ball very hard at the panel so that it hit the floor about a foot before the panel. The ball could ricochet off the panel, travel way up and over his head to a bounce far to his right, then return to his right hand to recover the juggling pattern.

Here's three tricks you can do using English.

Cascade three balls. Side snap one ball out to your left. Quickly take the two balls in your hands and use them as binoculars to scan the audience, then when the single ball gets back, recover the cascade.

Cascade three balls. Side snap one ball out to your left. While the ball is rebounding, shower the two balls until it gets back, then recover the cascade.

Cascade three balls. Side snap one ball out to your left, then take the two balls in your hands throw them straight down so they bounce right back up to your hands. When the single ball returns, recover the cascade.

STARTS

The Three Ball Bounce Start

Take all three balls in the right hand so that they form a triangle. Spread your fingers slightly so that the balls roll apart from one another. There should be about one quarter of an inch between each ball. Turn your hand over palm down so that your palm is parallel to the floor. Push your hand down, releasing the balls without any wrist action. Open your fingers wide so they do not interfere with the downward motion of the balls. You have to throw hard enough to make the balls bounce back up to chest high. The balls will hit, and bounce straight back up. As they pass your waist, snatch down on two of the balls. The single ball will continue up. Let it peak, then start the cascade by throwing from either hand. Be sure to keep the balls one quarter inch apart and throw with no wrist action or the balls may splatter when they hit the ground.

You can also use this technique bouncing the three balls under the leg. As the balls hit the floor, swing your leg over, snatch down on two balls, then start the cascade.

Once you have these moves down pat, try bouncing the three balls hard, snatch the two balls, do a pirouette, then begin the cascade.

The Three Over the Shoulder - Bounce Start

Take three balls in the right hand. Throw all three over the right shoulder with a snap of the wrist. As the balls pass by in front of you, catch the two outer balls, let the single one bounce, then go into the cascade.

The Three Over the Shoulder - Snatch Start

This is a slightly more difficult version of the previous start. You must move very fast. It begins the same by throwing three balls over the right shoulder. As soon as you release the balls, bring your hands up in front to quickly snatch down on the two lowest balls, then quickly get into the cascade before the single ball goes by. If, when you look up, there is only one low ball, grab it with the right hand, then throw it straight up in a center column or wherever there is a space, catch the two descending balls (as in one up - two up), then recover the cascade.

These same techniques work well if you throw three under the same or opposite leg, behind the back, or just straight up in front of you. A more difficult version of this is to throw the three balls through your legs and up over your back. Spread your legs about three feet apart. Without lifting your feet, bend forward reaching as far as you can, and throw the balls through your legs and high up and over your back. Straighten up to snatch the two lowest balls, then start the cascade.

The Three Over The Shoulder - Head Bounce Start

Bobby May used this start in his stage act for many years.

Toss the three balls over your shoulder. In time you will figure out how to get the balls to separate in mid air the way you want them to. It's a combination of wrist snap and finger movement that you can learn only with repetition. In any case, you want only one ball to go high so that the three balls form a triangle over your head. Snatch down on the two outside balls, let the single one do a head bounce, then start the cascade.

The Three Over the Shoulder - Neck Catch Start

This is a very popular three ball start. Toss three balls over the right shoulder, snatch down on the bottom two, then catch the single ball on the back of the neck. Do a high neck throw, then start the cascade. This also works well if you throw behind the back or under the leg.

The Three Ball Soft Toss - Leg Over Start

Put three balls in the right hand, palm up, so the triangle that the balls form is parallel to the floor. Loosen your grip a bit so that the balls drift slightly apart. Toss the balls lightly and let them hit the ground. They should hit in unison. As they fall, lift your right leg up and over, as the balls rebound, dip to one knee, snatch down on the outer two balls, then start the cascade after the single ball peaks.

Once you have control of the leg over start, try the same thing with a jump over. You have to time it perfectly and do the scissors jump quickly! Also try a three ball soft toss, pirouette, snatch two, then dip to the knee to cascade.

The Crossed Hands Start

This is an *Alan Howard* start!

Take two balls in your right and one in the left. Cross your right arm under the left and throw straight up with both hands. Uncross your hands, snatch the outer two balls, then start the cascade.

Three Over the Shoulder - Catch All Three

This is quite difficult. Toss three balls over the right shoulder. Work on your wrist action so that all three balls spread out in the air in a vertical column one ball above the other with as much space as possible between balls. It may take you some time before you get the hang of this . When the three balls line up, try to catch them all back in the throwing hand. You can cheat a little by snatching the bottom ball out of the air, or snatch which ever ball didn't line up vertically on the throw, then catch the other two.

Three Over The Shoulder - To Three in One Hand

If you can already do this trick, you don't need this book!

Put your left hand in your pocket. With the right, toss three balls high over the shoulder so that they line up as close to vertical as possible. As quickly as possible, snatch the bottom ball, throw it straight up and high, then quickly snatch the next nearest ball, also throw it straight up and high. Do the same with the last ball. If you snatch fast enough and get the balls to come back down at the right intervals, you should be able to keep the three balls going in one hand. I find it easiest to get into the three in one hand using columns.

Heel Kick Over the Shoulder Start

This trick is best learned with a sponge ball or a tennis ball. Place the ball between your heels so it touches the floor. Squeeze your heels together lightly, just enough to hold the ball snug. Jump up and forward, kicking your heels so as to throw the ball up and over your right shoulder. As you finish the kick, look to your right to catch the ball. You will have to twist your legs a bit to the right on the kick to get the ball up and over your right shoulder. To start the cascade, hold a ball in each hand. Do the heel kick and start the cascade with the right hand.

Once you are familiar with the various starting techniques you will have enough basic knowledge to invent your own starts.

FINISHES

The One Ball Catch Behind the Back

With one ball in the right hand, make an average height toss to the left hand. As the ball peaks, bring your right arm behind your back, twisting your torso to the right so that your right hand ends up in the approximate position where your left hand would be to make the catch. Now try the same trick to end the cascade. Pick any right hand ball and throw it over the top of the pattern toward a left hand catch. Catch the next ball coming to the right and quickly hand it off to the left. Reach behind your back to catch the ball thrown over the top in your right hand.

The Behind The Back Catch - Pirouette Out

This is the same trick just explained except you'll make a pirouette after the catch. Do the trick all the way to the catch, then stop. Your right arm is behind your back, your left arm is probably across your front, and your torso is twisted to the right. You couldn't be in a better position to start a pirouette. Unwrap your arms and untwist your torso, pushing off with your right toe. You will turn on your left foot. As you start to spin, pull your arms in tight. Spot with your head and step out of the pirouette after one turn. If you have any dance training, you should be able to easily make two or three turns.

The Under the Leg Catch

This is an easy finish that works the same as the behind the back catch. Throw any ball from the right up and over the pattern so that it comes down on your left side. Reach under the left leg to catch the ball just past your left thigh.

The Neck Throw to a Behind the Back Catch

This should be a fairly easy and consistent finish trick. Throw a ball to a neck catch. Do a neck throw so the ball goes straight up and off to the left. Reach behind the back with the right hand to make the catch, then pirouette out. You can also try neck throw to head bounce to behind the back catch, or neck throw to head bounce to floor bounce, jump over, behind the back catch.

The Through the Legs Catch

This is a very difficult finish trick that's hard to catch on a consistent basis, however, *El Gran Picaso* has been performing it for nearly twenty years with great results.

Take a ball in the right hand. Spread your legs about three feet apart and throw the ball over your head and behind you. Bend forward, reaching through the legs for the catch. This one is really hard to judge because the ball has to travel so far before the catch and you lose sight of it as soon as you bend forward. With a little practice you should be able to make the catch almost every time without looking.

Get the feel of this through the legs catch, then start a regular cascade. Throw one ball behind you, hand off the next ball that comes to your right hand, then reach through the legs for the catch. This trick is worth working on just for the thrill you'll get the first time you catch it!

The Neck Roll Down the Back

This finish is kind of similar to the through the legs catch. The last catch is made in the same way, however, instead of traveling through the air to the catch, the ball is caught on the neck, then rolls down the back to a through the legs catch.

It helps to wear a tight fitting shirt for this. If you're wearing a belt, take it off. Throw a ball to a neck catch. Lift your body to start the ball rolling. Keep your shoulders hunched and a slight arch in the back so that the ball rolls right down your spine. As it gets to your waist, bend back down and reach through the legs for the catch. You have to get the ball rolling fast enough to make it all the way down your back and over your back side, but not so fast that the ball gets there before your catching hand does.

After a few days you will know by feel where the ball is on your back and be able to adjust the catch timing accordingly. For a really easy finish, get a top hat, derby hat, or any hat with a strong brim. Try to incorporate the hat into your act some way so that you are wearing it for a reason during your routine. For a finish to do the neck catch, roll the ball down your back, and catch it through the legs in the hat. If your roll goes down the center of your back, it will be hard to miss your hat.

Three Balls Into a Hat From a Shower Bounce

Put on your hat and start a three ball shower. Tighten your pattern up, then in three consecutive throws, toss the first ball up and out of the pattern to a floor bounce about two feet to your left. Throw the next ball to the same height and to a floor bounce in front of you, and the last ball to a floor bounce about a foot to your right. Make these throws quickly and close together, take off your hat and catch each ball from left to right after it's first bounce.

The High Throw Bounce to Hand Trap

This is one of *Paul Bachman's* favorite finishes.

Take a ball in the right hand and throw it straight up to about six feet above your head. Aim the ball so that it comes down just a few inches in front of your right shoulder. Let it fall to a floor bounce. Stand erect with your right arm straight at your side. On it's way to the floor, the ball should pass just an inch or so from your right hand. As soon as it passes, bend your wrist back and open the hand so that the ball bounces off the floor and smacks to a catch in your hand.

Since the path of the ball after it bounces is predictable, you can easily make the catch without looking. When you do this for an audience, make the high throw, then get into your erect position with the right arm stiff at your side. Look up at the ball as it peaks, then keep looking up as the ball passes in front of you. The audience will think you missed it, and expect it to bounce very high after such a high throw. They will be surprised when you trap it in your hand.

THREE

ROUTINE

How to Structure a Routine

Many jugglers just juggle for recreation, usually in a park or a gym, with casual onlookers. In this situation it doesn't much matter what kind of tricks you do or how you arrange them. You are juggling simply for your own enjoyment and don't need to be concerned with entertaining those around you.

If you plan to show your skills on a more formal level for the enjoyment of others, there are a number of guidelines you can follow so that you can construct a routine of your best tricks arranged in an order that allows your audience to understand and appreciate what you are doing.

If you are performing for jugglers I would say do every variation of every trick that you can think of arranged in order of difficulty, executing each trick with first the right hand, then the left hand, and finally both hands. Jugglers will sit for hours to watch and appreciate every subtle variation. A non juggling audience will not. You have to bring the art down to their level and cater to a rather short attention span.

One of the first articles I ever saw about juggling was in an old copy of the I.J.A. Newsletter. A retired professional was giving tips on public performance. It went something like this.

The audience, in general, doesn't know exactly what tricks you are doing. They are watching you to entertain themselves and will lose interest the moment you allow them to. Therefore it is important to arrange your tricks in an order so that each trick you do is as different as possible from the previous one. In that way, even though the audience doesn't know precisely what you were doing in your last trick, they know they are seeing something completely different now!

The article went on to suggest arranging tricks in order of the position of the pattern. Start with a middle trick, then do a high trick, then a low trick. I would say start out with three or four tricks of pretty basic "in front of the body" juggling, and go on to feature a variety of tricks from various categories, broken up by and ending with a sustained turning trick. I would not go for longer than three minutes without at least changing props. I don't care how good a juggler you are. You're pushing your luck if you continue beyond three minutes of straight juggling.

Choice of tricks is very important. It's only natural to want to save what you think to be your greatest tricks for last. Successful professional entertainers always think from the audience's point of view. You will always hear the pros say "that's a great audience trick". The difficulty of most juggling tricks goes completely unnoticed by an audience, unless you present the trick in a manner which, in the guise of entertainment, educates them to it's intricacy and makes them respond with appreciation. Audience response to a trick is priority one! Try each trick out to see which ones get the best reaction, then arrange them accordingly saving the best "audience trick" for last.

Music is an important ingredient to a good routine. Pick a three minute piece that has a strong, definite beginning and ending, and a tempo that you can match up with at various points of your routine. Map out your routine on paper to get an idea of how the tricks are going to flow. Look for music that has varied passages and a flow similar to your routine.

Here's another important point worth mentioning. If you are performing in public, show only the material you can do with confidence on a consistent basis. Do a controlled, neat show with as few unplanned catastrophes as possible so the audience goes home with memories of a GOOD JUGGLER, not a lousy one. Save your questionable tricks for the gym!

SUGGESTED ROUTINES

If you learn all of the tricks mentioned in this book, you will have enough repertoire to construct a number of first class three ball routines. Here are three suggested routines of varied difficulty.

Note that when I say "direct" I mean to recover the cascade by making as few throws as possible, then get quickly into the next suggested pattern. With practice you will eventually be able to transfer directly from one pattern to another without throwing any cascade throws in between.

Confident Beginner

Throw one ball under the leg into a regular cascade : half shower with right hand : back to cascade : half shower with left hand : back to cascade : one up - two up for six throws : one up - two up cross for three throws : back to cascade : under the leg throw right : under the leg throw left : color ball alternating under left and then right leg for six throws : high throw to floor bounce, pirouette, then recover cascade : short toss to floor bounce right leg over : forced bounce cascade on floor for ten throws : back to cascade : up to over head cascade : back to cascade : random behind the back throws right : random behind the back throws left : back to cascade : three ball shower turning to the left for one revolution : back to cascade : throw one ball over the top to behind the back catch in the right hand - **END**

Intermediate

Three over the shoulder, catch two, let one bounce start : cascade : one up-two up twice : one up-two up-cross twice three ball shower : three ball shower, pass one behind back three times : three ball shower over the shoulder : back to cascade : through the pattern back and forth : through the pattern up and around : ball on the string : random place rolls on the head left and right : two in one hand around the head : tick-tock six times : light toss one ball to floor bounce leg over, to knee bounce back to floor bounce, jump over : squat to knee to recover cascade : stand up to over head cascade : down to "solid" claws right, then to "solid" claws left, then "solid" claws both hands : three ball drop : back to cascade : to forced bounce shower on floor : to forced bounce cascade on floor with random under the leg throws : back up to cascade : to three in one hand : to "solid" back crosses with right, then "solid" back crosses with left, to "solid" back crosses both hand : back to cas-cade : to neck catch : neck throw to behind the back catch in right hand - **END**

Professional

Three over the shoulder start: cascade for two throws: one up pirouette : one up pirouette : direct to reverse cascade : one up - two up three passes : direct to half turn throwing one ball : half turn back throwing one ball : half turn throwing three balls : half turn back throwing three balls : direct to shower turning to your left one revolution : reverse direction shower : one between two to the count of eight : one up pirouette : two up pirouette : three up pirouette : "solid" right hand throws under right and left leg : direct to behind the back cascade on the left side : to behind the back cascade alternating left and right sides : floor bounce shower : direct to forced bounce floor cascade : to forced bounce floor cas-cade with right throws alternating under right and left legs turning left for one revolution : back up to regular cascade : to neck catch : to head bounce : to knee bounce : to floor bounce right leg over : direct to second floor bounce jump over : to regular cascade on one knee : rise throwing one high to over head cascade : gradually lower over head cascade in front of you turning into "solids" clawing with both hands, faster, faster, faster : "solids" shoulder throws with both hands turning to your left for one revolution : back to regular cascade : direct to one over the top to behind the back catch : dou-ble pirouette out   - **END**

"JOGGLING"

The sport of "joggling" is steadily gaining popularity among jugglers. "Joggling" is combination of juggling and running that has grown to become a very important event at the various juggling competitions and has most recently gained international recognition since a great many "jogglers" have competed in the Los Angeles, New York, and Boston Marathons.

If you would like more information about "joggling", contact:

Bill Giduz - Editor
Juggler's World Magazine
Box 443
Davidson, North Carolina 28036

MASTERING THE HEADROLL

Dick Franco - Hansa Theatre Hamburg 1979

FOREWORD

By **Kit Summers**

Most people define juggling as the manipulation of three or more objects, but juggling even a single object can be very entertaining. The head roll is a great example of this. It is an up and coming trend among jugglers, so to see such detailed instruction on it at this time is most appropriate. The head roll is not a new trick! It was first made popular back in the time of Henry the VIII. He was quite well known for this!

Audiences are always impressed when they see a person throw a ball up to a forehead balance, then when the ball is rolled from ear to ear, they are overwhelmed. This is a trick that you can practice anywhere, anytime. If done correctly, it looks as if you are doing a magic trick. To the audience, it seems impossible that a ball could just be rolling around your head like that. Up until now there has not been any specialized instruction written on the head roll.

I feel that Dick Franco is a very qualified person to write on the subject. He really has the head roll down to an art. Since 1977 I have see Dick do the head roll in his act many times. He is a master of the trick. I think you will enjoy this instruction and find that the head roll will soon become part of your regular repertoire.

FOUR

MASTERING THE HEADROLL

INTRODUCTION

The head roll, or rolling a ball from ear to ear, must certainly be one of the best audience tricks of all time. Since learning it involves no toss juggling skill whatsoever and only a slight knowledge of balance, the head roll is an ideal trick for not only jugglers, but also comedians, magicians, and the neighborhood show off! I have personally used the head roll as a featured part of my act since the day I first learned it, and find in going back through the history of juggling that the majority of professional jugglers utilized this highly commercial trick in one form or another.

One of the earliest masters of this skill was the great Italian juggler, Enrico Rastelli who had total control of every conceivable variation of rolling an air filled ball on the head. Rastelli is still considered by jugglers to be the greatest juggler who ever lived, and was the one artist responsible for bringing juggling out of the circus side show and up to the level of fine art that it is considered today.

The only prop involved in learning the head roll, is one ball. It can be carried anywhere easily, ready to give you something to do when you have nothing, and ready for that unexpected opportunity to perform. With a little practice you will also be able to manage with certain out of round objects like apples, oranges, melons, or smaller objects like marbles or peas.

An other juggler who used this very commercial trick was *Bobby May*, considered to be the finest of the American jugglers, who specialized in using a smaller, hard rubber, lacrosse ball. *Francis Brunn* and *Rudy Cardenas* work with balls of various sizes, as do *Gus Lauppe, Rudy Horn,* and *Paul Bachman.*

The head roll is a very difficult trick to learn when compared to other juggling or balancing tricks, however, once you have perfected it, you will find it takes very little practice to maintain. I am sure that in time you will feel as I do and consider it to be one of your favorite tricks.

CHOOSING A GOOD PROP

For the fastest progress I suggest a small, hard, rubber ball measuring from 2 1/2 inches up to 3 inches in diameter. The ball should be perfectly round and fairly heavy with a smooth outer surface. Since you will be dropping it quite a lot at first, it would be a good idea to have a ball that bounces. It will save you from bending all the way down each time to pick it up.

EXAMPLES OF A GOOD PROP

1. lacrosse ball
2. solid rubber dog ball
3. billiard ball
4. wooden croquet ball
5. field hockey ball

The ideal prop, a lacrosse ball, is sometimes quite hard to find in the United States. If you have a large sporting goods store in your area, try to order one. There are two good brands, the best being VICEROY, a Canadian product, and an American version made by SPORT CRAFT. If you can't get anybody to order one for you, then try the pet shops for the unscented version of the doggie ball. I'll tell you ahead of time, the one with the bell will drive you nuts!

Unless you have no other choice, don't use a baseball, softball, tennis ball, or sponge rubber ball. A bowling ball is not much good either as it may eventually dent your head. Using them will make the beginning stages much more difficult, however, you will be needing a sponge rubber or tennis ball a little later in order to practice a few things that might be a little hard on your head with a heavier ball.

Let me mention as well that all stages of the head roll are best worked on in front of a large mirror. The mirror is especially important during the first five stages.

A Word About Practice

If you want to learn this trick in the least amount of time, I suggest that you practice three times a day, beginning with short sessions and gradually building up to about half an hour per session. In between sessions try to keep the ball handy for quick one minute sessions whenever you have the time. On a trick like this, practice sessions become unproductive after thirty minutes unless you spell them with other activity.

Concentration is also very important. After every few minutes of each session, stop and clear your head, then refocus your attention on what you are doing and start again. With these suggestions in mind, it is not unreasonable to expect fair control over all the aspects of the head roll outlined in this book within three weeks time.

The Forehead Balance

The first step toward learning the head roll will be the forehead balance. In teaching this, many times I have found that certain individuals have to work much harder than others simply because of the way in which the skin lies on their forehead. Persons with a deeply wrinkled brow can cheat a great deal by raising their eyebrows to form a tee for the ball to sit on. If you are so lucky to have a nice soft forehead, you will probably have this first move well under control in just a few minutes. Some people though, no matter how hard they try, cannot get enough wrinkle to make the ball stay put. So for those of you not so fortunate, you will just have to work a little bit harder at it.

Take a relaxed stance with feet slightly apart and knees slightly bent. Drop your head and upper body back, then place the ball on the center of your forehead, raising the eyebrows to give the maximum possible wrinkle.

NOTE:

The ball must go in the center of the forehead, above the eyebrows, NOT on the bridge of the nose.

Steady the ball with your finger until it stays balanced in one place. Try to keep it in this balanced position for about ten seconds, then take it off and straighten up. Those with a good wrinkle will probably have little problem with this. For those of you who don't, the balance will be more delicate. If the ball is rolling off your forehead and over your nose, which is usually the case, your head and body are not bent back far enough. If it rolls off and back over the top of your head, then you are bent back too far. Adjust your body position accordingly.

After the first few attempts, I am sure that you will feel quite strained holding this bent back position. This will pass in time and gradually you should feel more and more relaxed in this position.

Practice this balance until you can hold it under control for at least twenty seconds, then move on to the next lesson.

Forehead Balance Exercises

Try any or all of the following exercises to help develop a fore-head balance that you can put there and forget about! Once you have really mastered the balance, you will be able to take your eyes and concentration off of the ball and put them to use doing other things at the same time you are maintaining the balance.

1. While keeping your attention on the ball, place it in the balanced position, then every five seconds or so, shake your head very slightly left and right, and then up and down. Shake it just enough to make the ball move, but not so much as to lose the balance entirely. In between the shaking motion, try to maintain the balance. Do several repetitions of this exercise without losing the balance. This is also a very good pre show warm up if you happen to work professionally. If you are using the wrinkle method, keep your wrinkle as deep as possible.

2. With your attention on the ball, place it in the balanced position with the forehead wrinkled as much as possible. Slowly unwrinkle your forehead until the ball is in a pure balance. To do this you have to constantly adjust your head position in order to keep the ball in the middle of your forehead. These adjustments are very fine and take some time to develop fully, so be patient. Hold the pure balance as long as you can, then go back to the wrinkle. Repeat this cycle until you can go through it five times without losing the balance, lengthening the pure balance as you progress. Eventually you will be able to hold the pure balance indefinitely, when you are that good, try the first exercise without the wrinkle.

3. With the ball in the balanced position, maintain the balance while walking forward, then backward, and also side to side. Try bending down to your knees, then bend slowly back. Work your way down until you are laying flat on your back, then get back up again. If this is too easy for you, try mixing it with the first two exercises.

4. Repeat exercises 1, 2, and 3, only this time focus your eyes and attention on the ceiling throughout the duration of the exercise. Try not to look at the ball..... *feel the balance.*

5. Repeat exercises 1, 2, and 3 with eyes closed tight. Again *feel the balance.*

6. Place some objects, coins, keys, etc., in your right pocket. Focus your attention on the ceiling, then place the ball in the balanced position. Keep your eyes and attention on the ceiling! Take what is in your pocket with your right hand, pass it to your left hand and put it in your left pocket, then take it out and pass it back, all the while feeling the balance with eyes and concentration on the ceiling. Vary this exercise so you pass the object behind your back, under your legs, and over your head. When it passes over your head, take your eyes and attention off of the ceiling and onto the object. Focus on it and examine its every detail, then change your attention back and forth between object and ceiling, *feeling the balance!*

7. Try all of these exercises with eyes closed, but not near the pool.

8. Place a tennis ball on the floor about two feet in front of you. Put your balance ball in position, then bend down, pick up the tennis ball and stand back up. Try to keep half of your attention on the balanced ball and the rest of your attention on the general area in front and slightly above you. Put the tennis ball in your right hand, then throw it up in arc to a catch in the left hand. Repeat throwing the tennis ball back and forth, continuously sharing your attention between the tennis ball and the balanced ball. Next, try lifting the leg and throwing the tennis ball under it to a catch in the opposite hand.

Once you have gone through all of these exercises, I am sure you will know what I mean by *"feeling the balance."* This feeling is exactly the same as the automatic mode you are in while walking down the street. As long as you walk normally, you pay no attention to keeping your balance. The fine adjustments are made unconsciously, but should you trip or in some way suddenly lose your balance, all of your attention is immediately focused on correcting the situation. Once the problem is corrected, you go back on automatic. With diligent practice, the head balance can be the same.

Toss to the Forehead Balance

If you have spent some time and effort on all of the preceding exercises, your forehead balance should be really terrific by now, so lets go one step further and learn to toss the ball onto the forehead rather than just placing it there. When juggling, this is the smoothest and most effective way to get the ball to the forehead. You would throw a ball right out of the pattern to the forehead catch.

This is where your tennis ball will come in handy. Assuming that you are right handed, take the tennis ball in your right hand, get in the feet apart, knees bent stance, with the head and body straight up and down. Bring your right hand, palm up, about six inches in front of your chin, about chin high. Gently toss the ball in a straight line, directly at the center of your forehead. Just before it lands, bend head and body back slightly to absorb the impact of the ball. As you bend, wrinkle your forehead, and be sure to bend back far enough to properly balance the ball. The object of this is to have the ball meet your forehead with no rebound whatsoever. If the ball is bouncing off your forehead, your timing is wrong. You are starting back either too early, or too late, or else you are not moving fast enough. Adjust your movements accordingly until you get a nice soft contact. When the ball makes contact with your forehead, your head should be travelling back at about the same speed as the ball. Many jugglers are so adept at this that they can catch a raw egg that has been tossed up from the foot.

Work on this throwing from chin level, then as you get your confidence, throw from lower until you reach waist level. A good exercise is to bounce the ball on the floor, then sneak under it for the forehead catch.

Once you are no longer banging your head with the ball, switch to the lacrosse ball. If you are a juggler, try juggling three balls, then throw one right out of the pattern to the forehead catch. Throw the ball under the leg, behind the back, or bounce off the knee to the catch!

The hardest part about this trick is finding the proper timing between the throw of the ball and the contact point.

The Temple Balance

NOTE:
Find a large mirror.

The temple balance is much easier to learn if you practice in front of a mirror. Facing the mirror, take the heavy ball and bend at the waist far to the right. Look at yourself in the mirror so that your eyes and nose point directly at their reflection, and not at all towards the floor. Place the ball on your left temple then raise your nose until the ball rests gently against your ear. If the ball tends to roll over your ear lobe and down your neck, tip the top of your head down a bit more to correct this. If it rolls off the top of your head, your head is bent too far over, pull it up a bit. While working on this, straighten up often to clear your head, then try again until you can get the ball to stay put for at least ten seconds.

Next, bend over left and adjust your position until the ball rests gently against your right ear.

Once you can hold each side for at least twenty seconds, try shaking your head gently or walking while maintaining the balance. A good exercise is to alternate left and right ten second temple balances, for ten repetitions. This improves both sides uniformly and gives you the chance to straighten up in between.

Now take the ball in your left hand. Stand straight up and hold the ball against your left temple so that it touches your left ear. Bend quickly down to your right, glancing at the mirror to be sure your eyes and nose point directly to their reflection. As you reach what you think is the correct position in which to maintain the balance, let go of the ball. Repeat this procedure until you can quickly and consistently reach the perfect position. Work on both sides, then try alternating until you can quickly make ten perfect alternating repetitions.

As soon as you have descent control of the temple balance on both sides, try a throw to a temple balance. Start the same as you would for a throw to a head balance using a shorter throw at first. You may want to use the tennis ball again until you get your confidence with this. Throw just as if you are going for a forehead catch, but at the last second bend and turn the head left or right to a catch on the temple. Be sure to keep the ball in sight as you bend and use your ears to stop the roll of the ball.

The Roll Down

If you have well rehearsed the previous lessons, the roll down should come very easy, but don't get too excited, the roll up is much more difficult.

NOTE:

For the roll down portion of these exercises, be sure to make a clear area away from all the furniture. If you whack your head on something, you will have a lot of trouble getting the ball to roll over the bump! Chair backs are your worst enemy.

The first roll down will go to the right temple, so start in the forehead balance position and shift most of your weight over to your left foot. Snap your head and body down to the left temple balance position. Keep one eye on the ball and the other on the mirror so you can see if your down position is good.

NOTE:

The most common fault at this point is letting the nose drop. If you are having trouble keeping the ball resting against your ear, re-examine your basic positions in the mirror and make the necessary adjustments. After a few attempts, try to feel the ball as it rolls across your forehead and down to your temple. By feel, you will always know where the ball is even though you cannot see it. Sometimes you may have to bend slower to wait for the ball, or sometimes faster depending on how you start the ball rolling.

Practice the roll down on alternate sides until you have good control, then move on the the next lesson.

The Roll Up

As I mentioned before, the roll up is the most difficult part about learning the head roll. You have to rely a great deal on the feel of the ball to get the timing just right.

During the roll down, gravity starts the ball rolling as you bend down and out from under it. For the roll up, the ball is traveling up and against gravity, so you have to initiate that upward movement of the ball with body language.

Bend left to the temple balance position with knees well bent. Place the ball on the right temple and shift your weight slightly to the right. Dip the top of your head slightly so that the ball begins to roll toward the crown of your head. As the ball reaches the round part of your skull, stand up straight into the forehead balance position. The speed with which you stand up depends solely on how fast the ball is rolling towards the top of your head. Only you can judge this by the feel of the ball.

Experiment with this using different timing and body language until you find what is most comfortable, and what gets the best results. The timing between when you straighten the body and when the head snaps up is the most important. This timing will no doubt be quite erratic for a while until you get the feel of it. Sometimes if the ball is rolling too fast, you may have to shift your hips over to the other side in order to get your head back under the ball. The timing of the roll up and the roll down are rarely the same and will always require constant adjustments on your part, however, as you perfect it, these adjustments will be reduced to the point that they are not noticeable.

Probably the roll up will be the most frustrating of all the lessons. Don't get discouraged if it takes you a week or two to get it right on your good side. Your bad side may slow you down quite a bit as well. If you feel you have one side far superior to the other, go back to the basics and over practice your bad side. Start your practice sessions with your bad side and favor it until both sides are equal. Don't give up, you are almost there!

The Ear to Ear Roll

Now that you have fair control of the roll up and roll down on each side, put them all together into one successive exercise, holding the forehead balance and each temple balance briefly between each move.

Start with the forehead balance. Roll down and up on the right side for ten counts, then repeat with the left side. Once you can do ten counts each side without loosing the balance, try alternating left to right. When you have that, go for the ear to ear roll.

Start with the ball balanced on the left temple. Roll the ball up, non-stop over the forehead, then down to stop against the right ear. The most difficult part about this will be staying under the ball while shifting your weight in preparation for the roll down. This weight shift should occur just before the ball reaches the center of the forehead on the way up, then a slow roll across the forehead to allow you time to shift your weight, then a fast roll down to the ear. Remember to keep your nose and chin up for the roll down portion in order to coax the ball to roll to your ear.

Practice the ear to ear roll left to right for five or ten repetitions, then try right to left. Be sure to spend enough time on each side so that they both develop equally.

Once you have the roll from one ear to the other and stop, on both sides, try to go non stop from left to right, and back again. Then go for ten counts alternating non stop back and forth. Try to develop this into one smooth, continuous motion. Use your ears to bump the ball to change direction back up and over. Your goal is to develop a smooth, consistent rhythm. As your confidence improves, increase your speed.

The Pure Ear to Ear Roll

Now that you have the the head roll under your belt, don't get to thinking you are so tough. You have been cheating!!! The wrinkle on your forehead and the bumping of the ears is what makes the difference. Of course, for public performances it is always best to take the safe route on a trick like this as the audience really doesn't realize you are cheating. It probably even looks better to them rolling way down to your ears. If you really want to refine your head roll to point of perfection, unwrinkle your forehead and don't use your ears.

Let the ball roll only to your temples, using body language to make it change directions. Get your motion continuous to the point where there is no noticeable hesitations or breaks in rhythm. The ball should be moving up and down on a vertical line with your head and body pivoting smoothly beneath it.

The Flying Ear to Ear Roll

Another good way to refine your control over the head roll is to practice getting the ball from temple to temple without letting it touch the forehead on the way over. Start the ball rolling normally, as soon as it is on its way, duck out from under it and catch it on the opposite temple. Then fly it back to the other side. With practice, you will be able to perform this variation from side to side even faster that the conventional ear to ear roll.

The Bridge of the Nose Balance

Although probably not noticeable to an audience, the bridge of the nose balance is a good transitional move for the tricks mentioned in the following paragraphs. Place the ball in the curve where your forehead meets the bridge of your nose. The side to side balance is the only thing you will be concerned with here because your forehead and nose will keep the ball from rolling backward or forward.

When you have control of this, try rolling the ball from the forehead balance, to the bridge of the nose balance, hold it, then roll back up to the forehead. Try this move with both a lacrosse ball and a soccer ball.

The Eye to Eye Roll

NOTE:
This is probably not a good trick to try if you wear contact lenses! Also, use a light ball or a larger, air filled ball, NOT a lacrosse ball.

A good comedy move and one of the easier variations is moving a lacrosse ball from eye to eye. With the head in the proper position, it is very easy to keep the ball in one of your eye sockets. Roll it down from the forehead or temple balance to a balance on the bridge of the nose, pick an eye and drop the ball GENTLY into the eye sock-

et. It's a smart idea to close that eye before the ball gets there.
Next, try moving it from eye to eye by rolling it over the bridge of the
nose. When you are done moving it from eye to eye, try to get back
to the bridge of the nose balance, then roll back up to the forehead.
Also try to go right from the eye, back to the temple balance.

The Roll to the Mouth

Start with a clean lacrosse ball in the forehead balance, then
roll it down to the bridge of the nose. Tip the head forward slightly so
that the ball rolls along the bridge of the nose, over the tip, and into
your mouth. If you bite the ball, you can drop your head and look at
the audience. If you have the other two balls in your hand, survey
the crowd by using them as binoculars!! To get it back to your forehead, flick your head back and catch it just as if you were throwing it
from your hand.

The Roll on the Face

Here's another good soccer ball trick. Both *Rudy Cardenas*
and *Francis Brunn* use this trick in their act. From the forehead balance, roll the ball down to the bridge of the nose, then practice quick
side to side and circular rolls on the face. The ball should roll from
the nose to the right cheek, down and over the mouth, up to the left
cheek, and back to the bridge of the nose.

The Roll from Forehead to Nape of Neck

NOTE:
This is a good trick for either a lacrosse or soccer ball.
Place the ball in the forehead balance position. Roll it straight
over the top of your head and back down to the nape of the neck.
Feel the roll of the ball as it goes. As the ball reaches your neck,
bend forward quickly at the waist, raise your head, and hunch your
shoulders so as to form a pocket for the ball. If the ball won't stay
put, try bending over quicker, or farther, or raise the head and hunch
the shoulders a bit more.

Rolling the ball back up to the forehead is extremely difficult.
The system is the same as the roll up from the temple balance to the
forehead, only you can't see the ball when it comes from the back of

the neck. A mirror is not much good on this one, you will have to rely on feel alone. Start the ball rolling by dipping your head and body forward slightly, then use body language to get the ball up and over the top of your head. You have to feel the ball as it rolls over the top of your head toward your forehead, then at just the right moment, bend back and into the forehead balance. It will take a great deal of practice to get the timing just right on this one.

A second and maybe easier variation of this is going from the neck to the temple. *Bobby May* was a master of this move and could roll the ball round and round from neck to temple, roll across the forehead to the opposite temple, back to the neck, and then around again with very little hesitation. Start the ball rolling, turning it toward your temple with body language. Use the same method for getting it back to the neck. This easier version will still take a great deal of practice!

The Hoop Roll on the Forehead

If you feel confident with a lacrosse or a soccer ball, you may want to try something different. A hoop will roll as well from temple to temple. The easiest kind of hoop would be a large bicycle rim, or a rim with a wide flat edge. *Carter Brown* is an American juggler who specializes in an old form of juggling, using wooden bicycle hoops. He rolls them great distances over the floor in intricate patterns. He juggles them in the air as well as rolling them around on his body. Carter has excellent control of rolling one of these large hoops from temple to temple.

It is possible to roll a regular thin juggling ring on the head as well, however, this is another trick that will take a lot of practice. You will have to learn three different PURE balances with the ring. The forehead, as well as both temples.

You could construct a ring that would be ideal for rolling. Make it about about ten inches in diameter and a little less than one inch wide with about a one inch grip. Paint it or add weight until it comes out around ten ounces. Decorate it with stripes so as to draw attention to the rolling motion.

Follow Up Ideas

Finally you have mastered the head roll! With a little more practice you can learn some other variations that might be useful. Put them all together and you can transform a short feature trick into a unique feature routine.

The Value of a Dent in the Head

Most people have dents in their heads. If you are a juggler, a dent in the head can be very important. I wouldn't suggest that you start whacking your head with a hammer to get a dent, however, if you already have one, why not take advantage of it if it's in the right place. *Bobby May* had a great dent on the top of his head. He could place a lacrosse ball there and forget about it. He could walk around, juggle, do just about anything he wanted with the ball just sitting up there. Bobby used this to great advantage in his act by placing a fourth ball in the dent and then juggle the other three. He would then roll the ball off his head and go right into a four ball juggle, or do the same from four to five balls. Bobby could also roll the ball right out of the head roll, up to the dent, then back into the head roll.

Feel around on the top of your head for any small indentations in the skull. Get in front of a mirror and put the lacrosse ball in the dent. Position your head until it stays put. With a little practice you should have no problem keeping it there. Walk around, bend, juggle, until you can feel the balance like second nature, then try to roll the ball from the dent down to the forehead or temple balance. If you think the dent is deep enough, try to roll the ball from the forehead balance back up to the dent.

Another variation of this trick was performed by the great Enrico Rastelli using a soccer ball. He would bounce the ball all over his body, knees, feet, head, and shoulders, then catch it in a forehead balance. From the forehead he would roll it up to a pure balance on the crown of his head, then walk in a square making ninety degree turns under the ball.

With a larger air filled ball, a dent in the head will not help you. For this you will have to develop a perfect, PURE balance. With a soccer ball or basketball, get in front of a mirror. Set the ball on the top center of your head, use your finger tips to steady it until you get the feel of the balance. Once you can balance it while looking in the mirror, try it without. If you roll your eyes up, you can probably see the edge of the ball, if it is big enough. This will help a great deal. If the ball is too small to see, then you will have to rely on feel alone.

CONCLUSION

Of course I haven't covered every trick that exists with three balls or the head roll. There is an infinite number of variations to be discovered yet, so use your imagination to invent some tricks of your own. If you have enjoyed yourself thus far and want to learn more about juggling, try the following title written by **Dick Franco** and available from:

BRIAN DUBE' INC.
25 Park Place
New York, New York 10007
(212) 619-2182

"THREE CLUB JUGGLING"

An Introduction

In depth beginner instruction of the basic three club cascade, plus ten basic tricks, two fancy starts, two fancy finishes, and forty eight rare photographs!

Watch for future titles available soon by **DICK FRANCO**

PHOTO COLLECTION

Bobby May

For the past eighteen years I have been fascinated by the history of juggling, and dedicated to it's preservation. I have had the pleasure of seeing and meeting many great jugglers, and have had the opportunity to collect many interesting artifacts. On the following pages are some of the photographs I have collected during my career. Some are very rare items from **Bobby May's** personal collection! He enjoyed them for many years and would be happy for you to enjoy them too!

Paul Bachman - At His Absolute Best !

The Great Paul Bachman

Kris Kremo - Stardust Hotel Las Vegas 1987

Kris Kremo - Stardust Hotel Las Vegas 1987

Stan Cavanaugh

Max Moreland - Germany 1944

Mathieu

JOHN MC PEAK

John Mc Peak - Friedrichstadt Palast Berlin 1977

Fanny Baird

Grigori Popovich - Moscow Circus US Tour 1989
(photo by Bill Giduz)

Billy Ray

Albert Schweitzer

Michael Moschen
(Photo Jim Moore)

Dick Franco - Hansa Theatre Hamburg 1979

Dick Franco - Café Versailles New York 1982
(photo H. V. Francis)

Noel Franco

Bobby May - Capitol Theatre New York

Bobby May - Bringing Down the House In Lebanon

Bobby May - La Scala Theatre Berlin 1933

Bobby May

Winnie May - 1935
(Bobby May's sister)

Mark Nizer

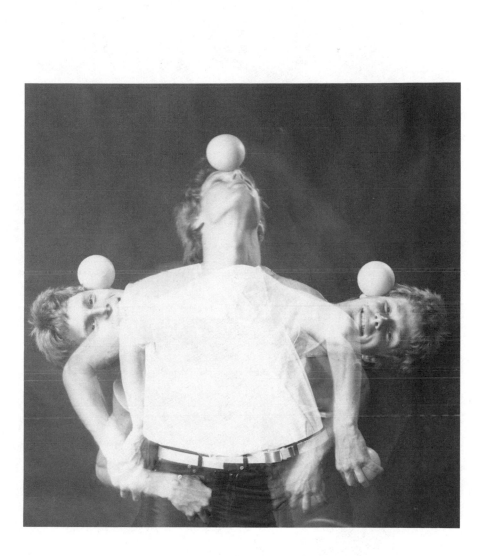

Mark Nizer

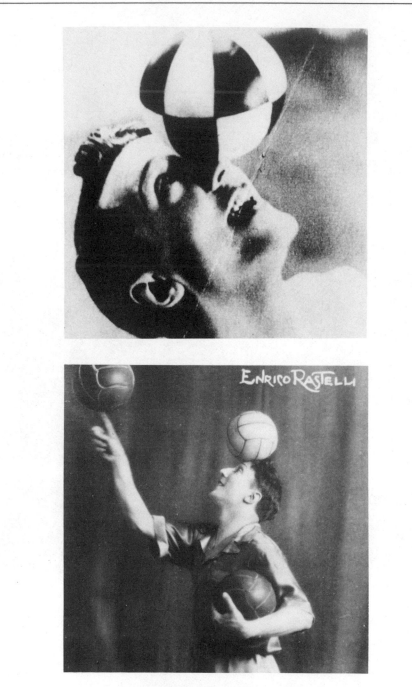

The Great Enrico Rastelli

Tod Paul Ding

Mardo

Wilfred Du Bois

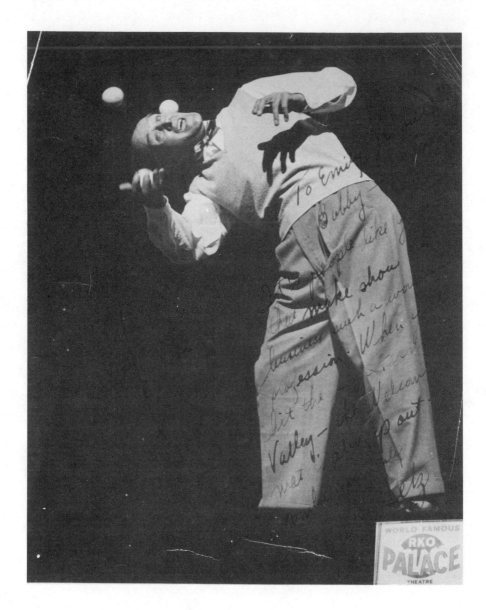

Val Setz

The Dedicated Alan Howard

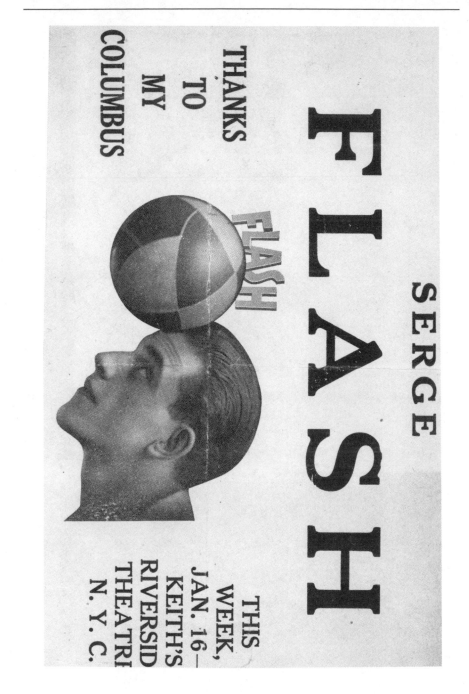

Serge Flash

Felovis

Dick Franco - Café Versailles New York 1982
(photo H. V. Francis)

Dick Franco - Hansa Theatre Hamburg 1979

Bobby May - Alhambra Theatre London

Bobby May - The International Juggler

Bobby May - Scala Theatre Berlin 1933

Bobby May - Or He May Not !

Bobby May - Capitol Theatre New York

Bobby May - The Life of the Party!

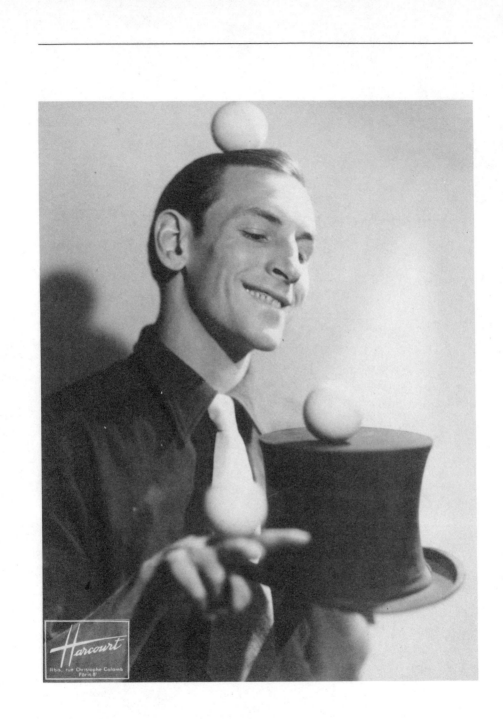

Bobby May

Bobby May

BRIAN DUBE

PRESENTS

Scene From "The Juggling Fool" - 1938

A GREAT AMERICAN JUGGLER

BOBBY MAY

A NEW VIDEO BY STEWART LIPPE

In 1987 I received a telephone call from Mr. Stewart Lippe. He said he was producing a film documentary on juggling and was looking for someone who had information about an old vaudeville juggler named **Bobby May.** Did he call the right place!

In the months that followed, Stewart spent hundreds of hours researching, filming, and editing material. The musical accompaniment to most of the originally silent juggling footage was completely re-recorded using **Bobby May's** original music scores that were written for those very routines.!

While going through some photographs we came across some old promotional shots of Bobby that appeared to have been taken on a movie set. With a little research we found out that Bobby had once been contracted by the Vita-phone Corporation to make a film short called "The Juggling Fool", in which he played a soda jerk who couldn't hold a job because he was hooked on juggling. The film was to have been used by cinemas to entertain the audience while the projectionist changed the reels of film for the main attraction. To my knowledge "The Juggling Fool" was never shown.

After many months of intense searching, Stewart finally located and obtained a copy of this extremely rare, never before seen film short. For the juggling world, "The Juggling Fool" has to be the "find of the century"! It's addition to the film "Bobby May - A Great American Juggler" has helped turn what was already a superb film, into an incredible historic masterpiece.

Dick Franco

Important Information

The International Juggler's Association is an organization devoted to the advancement of the art of juggling. The IJA's "Juggler's World" magazine which is published every other month, is an extremely valuable source of information. The IJA holds one major international convention each year as well as a great many smaller conventions and juggler meetings in both the USA and Europe.

For more information contact:

The International Juggler's Association
Richard Chamberlin, Secretary
P.O. Box 29
Kenmore, New York 14217

Two other great sources for juggling information are:

Up in The Air Magazine
127 Keefer Street
Ottawa, Ontario CANADA K1M 1N8

and

Kascade Juggling Magazine
Annastr # 7
D 6200 Wiesbaden, West Germany

END

(*actually, its just the beginning*)